MEMOIRS OF ALMOST BARREN WOMEN
OUR JOURNEY TO MOTHERHOOD

Written and Compiled by

Tanerra Willis BSN, RN, CPN

AMAZING FAMILY ENTERPRISES, LLC

MEMOIRS OF ALMOST BARREN WOMEN:
OUR JOURNEY TO MOTHERHOOD

Copyright © 2021

Paperback ISBN: 978-1-7342715-5-3

Hardcover ISBN: 978-1-7342715-4-6

ebook ISBN: 978-1-7342715-6-0

LCCN: 2021906777

All Rights Reserved. This book or any portion thereof may not be reproduced, stored, transmitted electronically, photocopied, or used in any manner whatsoever without the express written permission of the publishers except for use of brief quotations for a book review.

Printed in the United States of America.

Theamazingcorner

The Amazing Corner

www.theamazingcorner.com

amazingwethead@gmail.com

Editor: Steffanie Moyers
Formatted By: Farhan Shahid (fiverr.com/farhanshahid101)

MEMOIRS OF ALMOST BARREN WOMEN: OUR JOURNEY TO MOTHERHOOD

Dedication

This book is dedicated to my sisters, mother, and husband. To my sisters, your endless support and encouragement is irreplaceable. Your help has been the wind beneath my wings. At any given time, you have been my cheerleaders, editors, salesman, or focus group and I cannot thank you enough. I pray that when you see me it inspires you to be your best self without fear of failing. Thanks for riding with me and flying with me.

Mom, there is nothing like a mother's love. You showed me how to nurture, support, and celebrate a child. Through your example of love, I was able to propel into the mother and wife I am today.

To my husband, there are not enough words in the English dictionary to express my gratitude for your support and encouragement. You are the epitome of a good man and great father! I pray our son appreciates your guidance and influence. Each of you have added to my life greatly and I am forever grateful!

**MEMOIRS OF ALMOST BARREN WOMEN:
OUR JOURNEY TO MOTHERHOOD**

Special Thanks & Acknowledgements

Thank you for contributing your story:

- Geneva Miller
- Nicole Johnson
- Tanisia Murrell
- Robin Reaves
- Lindsey Oliver

You are all people of great strength! Through your transparent writings, each of you will be a catalyst in supporting and encouraging women and families on one of the toughest journeys of their lifetime. Please know that you are appreciated.

MEMOIRS OF ALMOST BARREN WOMEN:
OUR JOURNEY TO MOTHERHOOD

Contents

Dedication v

Special Thanks & Acknowledgements vi

Special Areas & Resources: viii

Foreword ix

Introduction 1

Chapter 01 | Infertility 3

Chapter 02 | A Look at Me 15

Chapter 03 | Challenges 23

Chapter 04 | Who Suffers from Infertility? 35

Chapter 05 | Infertility and Me 45

Chapter 06 | Releasing the Shame 63

Chapter 07 | Lessons Learned 75

Conclusion 81

Resources 89

Terms and Definitions 95

Works Cited 99

Journal 103

Reviews 157

MEMOIRS OF ALMOST BARREN WOMEN:
OUR JOURNEY TO MOTHERHOOD

Special Areas & Resources:

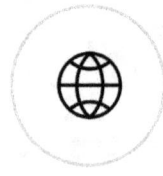

Support Groups/ Websites

Social Media

Terms

References

Foreword

MEMOIRS OF ALMOST BARREN WOMEN:
OUR JOURNEY TO MOTHERHOOD

I have learned that the greatest salve for grief is empathy. We seek it sometimes without even knowing that we're doing so. When the loneliness of our feelings begins to overtake us, having someone say, "I see you and you are not alone," is like finding a spring of cool water in a desert. For me, and I'm sure many others, *Memoirs of Almost Barren Women* will become that water.

When Tanerra reached out to me about reviewing the book and providing a foreword, I was honored and intimidated. I'm not often at a loss for words, but infertility is such an intimate and personal journey that I was somewhat uncomfortable with being a judge of how someone else has experienced it. But I'm so glad I answered her call. It gave me an opportunity to be a part of something special and profound.

Tanerra, and the brave women who boldly share their stories throughout these pages are mirrors and windows into the unspoken feelings of so many in the fertility fight. We fear that the actions of our pasts have caused the present. We worry that our relationships are ill-equipped for this. We wonder if the final answer to all our desires will be "no," we listen to friends and family members ask us intrusive questions or make judgments without context. We worry that we'll never be able to provide a sibling for the child we may already have.

Clearly, as you'll see from the stories found in this book, reproductive health education is different from sexual education. Many of us first learn about the real inner workings of our bodies when we encounter infertility. We may suffer with unruly menstrual cycles or uterine pain for years without ever knowing that it is abnormal. We don't talk about these things. We stuff them down and we go to work and church. We push through and even excel

MEMOIRS OF ALMOST BARREN WOMEN:
OUR JOURNEY TO MOTHERHOOD

---

in our personal and professional lives, all while carrying an intense emotional weight. It's a heartbreaking cycle of abuse that is exacerbated by the fact that so many of us feel like we have no choice but to suffer in silence. It is my hope that through these pages, you or someone you know will walk away equipped to help dismantle the cycle.

In my decade of infertility advocacy, I've waited for there to be more books that speak to the experience of black women and our unique corner of this space. We deserve to be heard, validated, and supported through the rough terrain of infertility. Thank you Tanerra for providing a resource that does just that.

Regina M. Townsend, MLIS
Founder
The Broken Brown Egg, Inc.

Introduction

MEMOIRS OF ALMOST BARREN WOMEN:
OUR JOURNEY TO MOTHERHOOD

If you are reading this book, you are probably a woman on a journey to become a mother. You may also be a man looking to support, understand, or encourage your partner on this journey. Lastly, you may be in a support role like a friend, a doctor, or in the behavioral health field looking to gain more understanding about women who walk this path.

Well, you have come to the right place. My goal is to share the bare truth regarding my journey. In Memoirs of Almost Barren Women you will learn about all my contributing factors, my challenges, my tears and my triumphs that contributed in this journey.

My story in no way reflects the ever-growing reasons for infertility or mothering challenges, but instead it displays my understanding and empathy of women/families who long to be parents. It shares in the pain, disappointment, shame, grief and fear a woman feels along the way.

It also encourages families seeking to be parents to accept where they are, avoid blame and shame, and embrace the many ways to celebrate caring for a life that is yours! I also purpose to support women and families who have varying circumstances. Therefore, I have asked a few friends to share their stories as well.

If you are about to embark on this journey to learn more about my story, I welcome you. I welcome you to find a quiet place, journal along the way, and remember you are AMAZING just the way you are. Infertility, miscarrying, and death of a child is painful! We don't always understand it and it often results in a "why me" position.

You can have what you desire! However, you may need to take an entirely different path than you planned. I pray this book brings you some relief and comfort and propels you to continue your journey to your heart's desire, embracing new paths to becoming a parent or gaining new understanding of those you support.

Love,

Tanerra

CHAPTER 01

Infertility

MEMOIRS OF ALMOST BARREN WOMEN:
OUR JOURNEY TO MOTHERHOOD

> Don't expect anyone to understand your journey, especially if they've never walked your path.
>
> **UNKNOWN**

Infertility plagues more women than we know. For many women it is our biggest secret. We keep it a secret for many reasons. For me it was embarrassment, self-blame, and shame.

According to the Centers of Disease Control, infertility is defined as not being able to get pregnant (conceive) after one year (CDC.gov, 2020), but to a women it means so much more. For me infertility meant sadness, despair, loneliness, limitations, guilt, and pain.

Unfortunately, for the larger portion of women with difficulties conceiving this issue torments us for much longer than a year. Sadly, for some, it will be with them for the remainder of their lives.

I am sharing my journey with you in hopes that infertility will only be a portion of your story and not the conclusion. If you have decided to end the quest to become a parent, I understand that as well. This topic is one that comes with a heavy weight that is very hard to bear. The great thing is you are not alone and there are so many paths to becoming a mother.

In this book you will read about the details of how I succeeded in becoming a parent. You will also hear from my friends and how they came to be called mom, mama, or mommy.

MEMOIRS OF ALMOST BARREN WOMEN:
OUR JOURNEY TO MOTHERHOOD

Each journey was completely different, but came with its own challenges, pain, and a different ending. Overall, each woman is able to share a message of hope and inspiration.

We also aim to encourage you as you traverse your own journey. We provide our stories as a means for different options for you to consider during your own walk. Ultimately, we are all in different stages and phases of this journey, and we also have diverse comfort levels with treatment options and desires to parent through atypical methods.

So, as you read, I also encourage yourself to exercise self-care. Journal throughout the way, draw, take walks. Prioritize you in a way that allows you to decompress the impact of this walk.

For the partners, continue to leverage separate realities. Be in the moment and allow grace and space as needed. You will never get it exactly right, but communication, connection, and presence mean more than you will ever know.

There are no perfect words, but say "I hear you, I am here, and we will get through this together." Ask questions without blame. Plan nights out and highlight your love and commitment to one another. Remember to share your authentic feelings as well. We need to know how you feel about it too.

The pain of infertility can be isolating. Even in your own home with a spouse/partner nearby. Men especially swallow their feelings and suppress them for many reasons. Your impact should be shared.

We thank you and need your support. You matter.

MEMOIRS OF ALMOST BARREN WOMEN:
OUR JOURNEY TO MOTHERHOOD

I love that you are my person and I am yours, that whatever door we come to, we will open it together.

A. R. ASHER

MEMOIRS OF ALMOST BARREN WOMEN:
OUR JOURNEY TO MOTHERHOOD

Tanisia's Journey

"I never imagined at 44, I would be single, barren, and fighting to preserve my fertility until I get married."

MEMOIRS OF ALMOST BARREN WOMEN:
OUR JOURNEY TO MOTHERHOOD

It is the melting of my heart as I think about the beauty and wonder of growing and bearing life inside my womb. The realization that only the hand of God could have designed such a miracle inside these flawed bodies.

As long as I can remember, I wanted to be a mother with a deep abiding desire to birth some children and adopt or foster others. To have a full, noisy, and beautifully messy home full of laughter, joy, and love. I have had dreams about it, my heart has ached for it, and I have desperately cried out in prayer to God. See, I grew up one of four children and if my mother had her way there would have been many more of us.

Unfortunately, after the birth of my youngest brother my mother had an emergency hysterectomy and lost one of her kidneys. This after being told by doctors to terminate her pregnancy to save her own life. That is the example of motherly love and sacrifice in which I was raised. It only further nurtured the desire I believe God knitted into my heart. It felt like it was my training ground, so surely this must be in God's plan for me.

I never imagined that at 44, I would be single, barren, and fighting to preserve my fertility until I get married. See, I believe in God's design for marriage and family. Some have asked if I would consider trying to have a baby on my own. It is something that I don't believe God is calling me to do but rather to wait for the promise. The promise is something that I believe God made to me after a season of prayer and fasting. Placing my petition before God about marriage and a baby. I remember the Lord clearly answering, "Yes!" That was 5 years ago and counting.

When I was 14 years old, I began having issues with extended heavy periods and daily migraine headaches. The doctor's solution was to put me on birth control pills which I took until I was about 25.

MEMOIRS OF ALMOST BARREN WOMEN:
OUR JOURNEY TO MOTHERHOOD

I am a Christian and accepted Christ at an early age but really got serious about being a true follower of Christ in my 20's. I made a rather culturally unpopular decision, but a God honoring decision to practice sexual purity.

Since I was no longer sexually active, I decided to stop taking birth control pills. I was also beginning to focus on my health and take a more holistic approach which meant stopping unnecessary pharmaceutical medicine. As my body adjusted to no longer taking hormones my periods normalized for about a year and then my life turned upside down. Hot flashes, acne, weight gain, hair loss, facial hair, and hyperglycemic moments became constant struggles.

My gynecologist at the time was very dismissive of my concerns about what was happening to my body. I began doing my own research, and I ran across an article about Polycystic Ovary Syndrome. As I read the list of 13 common symptoms, I realized I had 10 out of the 13 listed. When I approached my doctor about it, she disregarded my concerns and began telling me that at 28 years old my fertility would begin rapidly declining in the next year anyway. At that moment I was infuriated and made the decision to fight for my own health and fired my doctor.

After much research and personal recommendations from friends and family, I had finally found a new doctor. My first visit with Dr. Whitney was amazing, she listened to all my concerns and did some testing. I was diagnosed with PCOS (Polycystic Ovary Syndrome). It's a condition that can cause infertility and a host of other health conditions, including cancer and heart disease.

MEMOIRS OF ALMOST BARREN WOMEN:
OUR JOURNEY TO MOTHERHOOD

At 28 I was dealing with the threat of infertility and the potential for other life-threatening health conditions. I cried for weeks and battled depression at the thought that I may never be able to have children or worse die prematurely.

How could this be happening? I come from a family of very, very fertile women. Despite my mother's challenges with her last pregnancy, getting pregnant, carrying to term, and delivering her babies were not difficult. All of my aunties and cousins all talked about how fertile they were and had multiple pregnancies. I always assumed that I would be no different and having a baby would be easy.

All of those thoughts flooded my heart and mind. It caused my heart to ache even more and question God's goodness and love. **Why me?** Why do I have to be the one with fertility issues? Then I decided to fight and focus on my health with fitness and nutrition. Dr. Whitney was very encouraging and gave me hope that focusing on my nutrition could help rebalance my hormones and preserve my fertility. In just a few weeks my cycle normalized, and my symptoms went away.

Over the last 15 years, I have also been diagnosed with fibroids in addition to the PCOS. Grateful that they have not grown or caused any issues, but their presence threatens the opportunity for a healthy pregnancy.

Every year that has rolled by with no progress toward marriage, I find myself fighting fear, anxiety and depression that I may miss my opportunity to carry and birth a baby.

MEMOIRS OF ALMOST BARREN WOMEN:
OUR JOURNEY TO MOTHERHOOD

In 2018, while serving on the mission field in Kenya, I began having a very heavy period that lasted for five weeks. When I arrived back in the United States, I immediately went to my doctor to discover I had a large cyst growing on my left ovary and would need surgery to remove it. It was at that moment my gynecologist suggested that I see a reproductive endocrinologist. I loved that she understood and cared for my desire to give birth someday.

I went through a thorough fertility evaluation to potentially freeze my eggs. The outcome was another diagnosis, severe stage three endometriosis, polyps in my uterine cavity, confirmed a second fibroid in my uterine wall, and an adhesion band. My heart just broke as the doctor explained my condition and options for moving forward. I remember her excitement that in spite of everything going on I had better than average follicle egg count for a woman my age (42) with multiple issues.

I chose to have corrective surgery to preserve my fertility, praying that my left ovary would be okay and no scarring in my tubes. Awakened from surgery that took a little longer than expected to learn that the doctor was successful in removing the cyst from my ovary, leaving it intact. My uterine cavity was clear and healthy from the polyps and adhesion band.

The doctor was confused and couldn't explain what happened to the polyps and adhesion. I explained it was all God. We decided to leave those fibroids in place since they were small and would not hinder a pregnancy but removing them would limit my future birthing options. My heart rejoiced at the news and was excited to move forward with the egg freezing process until I learned that my insurance would not cover it unless I had a cancer diagnosis.

MEMOIRS OF ALMOST BARREN WOMEN:
OUR JOURNEY TO MOTHERHOOD

Cancer diagnosis! Really? The out-of-pocket cost was exorbitant and had to make a decision about taking on thousands of dollars of debt. I remember praying about the next steps and hearing God say, "Stop, just trust me! This is as far as you go in this process." It was with a heart full of ache and fear but a reckless abandon to trust God in that moment regardless of what science says and what my eyes could see.

Today, I reflect on this journey that God has entrusted to me. I am grateful that God has given me the opportunity to mother twice, children born in my heart. Once raising my nephew and again when I had the privilege to take in a teenage girl from my church. I recognize that in this season of waiting, God granted me beautiful opportunities to be a mother. Serving others in moments of their greatest and most pressing need. What I am learning is that God has given me a heart and passion to "mother on mission."

> Pure and undefiled religion before our God and Father is this: to care for orphans and widows in their distress, and to keep oneself from being polluted by the world.
>
> **JAMES 1:27**

Today, I am still awaiting the promises of God for a husband and a baby. I believe in God, period! He has never failed me yet, so I continue to rejoice and find contentment every day. In the meantime, I want my life to be full of sweet fruit by moving fully in my God given purpose and calling. Yes, that includes mothering. Refusing to allow myself to be stalled and stuck in the pain that barrenness can cause.

MEMOIRS OF ALMOST BARREN WOMEN:
OUR JOURNEY TO MOTHERHOOD

So, I am "Mothering on Mission" and preparing to open my home to foster with an openness to adopt. I wholly believe in God and trust His greatest and best plan for my life. That includes bearing or not bearing children, but I know He has prepared and called my heart to mother.

As I write this letter my heart presses into the presence of God pushing past the fear of news that my doctor just delivered. My ovarian reserve has drastically declined from a year ago. In this moment, I cling to the truth that God is the giver of life not science. That he has opened barren wombs many times before and He can do it again.

I am resting in truth! Truth is always the basis for trust and trust is always the basis for rest. Trust and rest grow on a steady diet of God's word!

Rest in the truth that we are image bearers of God, uniquely designed for good works, and His glory. Know that you have been trusted with a special journey that will bring life, light, and truth if we trust God's plan. His love for you and I is unmatched, incomparable, reckless, and a never-ending pursuit of our whole heart. I am barren, but not broken. I am living a bountiful life!

Tanisia

CHAPTER 02

A Look at Me

MEMOIRS OF ALMOST BARREN WOMEN:
OUR JOURNEY TO MOTHERHOOD

And you begin again.

Sometimes you lose, sometimes you win.

But you begin again.

Even though your heart is breaking, in time, the sun will shine.

BARRY MANILOW

When I first started to write this book it was 2011. This goes to show how hard it is to discuss this topic. It takes bravery and balls. It takes the desire to share with others what you have held close to your heart for so long. Infertility is something many of us carry as "the big secret."

I've never told anyone everything no matter how close we were. From my perspective people really didn't fully understand and to be honest I was not ready to be that open.

Initially, I was very sensitive about the subject. A few select people knew what was happening, but they didn't know my deepest and most intimate feelings. **No one felt what I was really feeling**. No one truly understood. When I think of why I held back, it was my own personal shame, guilt and fear.

If you are anything like me there are many things, moments, and feelings regarding your desire to conceive. In addition, the pain of not

MEMOIRS OF ALMOST BARREN WOMEN:
OUR JOURNEY TO MOTHERHOOD

conceiving leads you to keeping things to yourself. Of course, you tell this person this and that person that, **but you never tell anyone everything.**

At least that was the truth for me. I kept things from my husband because I felt he wouldn't understand or did not care as much as I did. I kept things from my parents because of embarrassment and their comments made me feel uncomfortable. I would only share parts of my story with my friends because of those ugly words **shame, guilt, and fear.** I also didn't want to be judged and/or pitied.

Here I was, in my mid-twenties. I was a married, degreed homeowner. It was only natural that the next step would be parenthood. I was married for two or more years and started to think of having a baby with my loving husband.

I always knew I wanted a family and to get it I sacrificed a lot and worked hard. Only to realize after trying for years that my previous bad decisions and thoughtless behaviors would come back to haunt me. It was immaturity, lack of knowledge, and limited guidance that I attributed to my actions.

Growing up all of my friends and cousins had boyfriends and long-term relationships and I was usually single. It was funny, I never saw a relationship that I envied or wanted to model my relationship after, yet I yearned for one. It wasn't long before loneliness led to me engaging in practices and relationships I would grow to regret.

MEMOIRS OF ALMOST BARREN WOMEN:
OUR JOURNEY TO MOTHERHOOD

Eventually, I figured it out but, in many respects, it was too late. That, of course, was realized in hindsight. After years of not conceiving, thousands of dollars of fertility care, millions of tears, and a looming cloud of isolation I realized that I got my act together and displayed my self-worth a decade too late.

I finally realized after dating the wrong guy yet again, I was focused on the wrong things as a young lady. I wanted companionship and I was looking for my knight in shining armor, but yet I was dating the guy who gave me squeals and thrills. These same guys gave me heartache, false hopes, and let down after let down.

The charade ended when I walked away from Mr. Wrong for the last time. The conversation ended with him asking me why I did not tell him to do the right things with his life and make better judgements. It wasn't until then that I realized that I spent my late teens and young adult life chasing my now and forgetting my future.

I neglected my body, emotions, and my future by causally sharing myself with men who I knew could not and would not be what I wanted in a spouse or the parent of my future children. It was these decisions and more that I truly believe contributed to my infertility struggles. It was these actions and inactions that led to me carrying shame and guilt related to my inability to bear children with my deserving husband.

In this book, I will share all of my perceived contributory factors of barrenness. I realize your story may be different. For some, it could be related to genetics or come as a result of an acquired illness. No matter the reason we can carry shame and guilt. We all wonder **why me and what if?**

I have finally released the shame. I pray you have, or you will too. **You are not alone**, and you can still have hope, joy, and motherhood.

MEMOIRS OF ALMOST BARREN WOMEN:
OUR JOURNEY TO MOTHERHOOD

Geneva's Journey

> My marriage suffered, my faith suffered, and I didn't share any of my emotions fully with my spouse.

MEMOIRS OF ALMOST BARREN WOMEN:
OUR JOURNEY TO MOTHERHOOD

I was upset with God and I was not going to New Year's Eve service on December 31st, 2017. I didn't feel up to worshipping. The year before I got married and we found out I was pregnant on our honeymoon. What a great surprise! I already had two children before this marriage, so I was not thinking about having a miscarriage. I never researched miscarriages or knew anyone who had them except my mother.

Fast forward to my first doctor's appointment. My husband and I were so excited, but I knew something was off because I felt "weird" that morning. As I laid on the table and the physician looked at the monitor, she said to us, "I am sorry, but I do not see a heartbeat." The fetus had stopped growing at nine weeks and I was supposed to be twelve weeks at that point in time. **All I remember was feeling like a failure**. I felt like I let my husband down because I lost his first child and I failed myself. How could I not carry this child in marriage when I had the other two children outside of a marriage? To be honest with you I don't think I ever really healed from that loss. I moved on and we tried to get pregnant again.

We were successful again without any help! This time I switched physicians' offices because I was not satisfied with the previous office. I went to get an ultrasound again and I was advised that everything was okay. I had a small amount of bleeding during the next day and was advised to go back for another ultrasound. My husband met me at the hospital and the technician said amongst many things, "I don't know why they told you that, there is no heartbeat. You can always try again." This time it hurt a bit worse because I had my older children with me, and they cried as well. Have you ever seen a family movie where someone passes away and the family is in the waiting room devastated? Well, that was us. Again, I was a failure and I had let my husband down.

MEMOIRS OF ALMOST BARREN WOMEN:
OUR JOURNEY TO MOTHERHOOD

I also carried around grief from telling my friends that I was pregnant and taking them through another loss with me. I realized that I didn't like feeling like the victim. I didn't want people to have pity on me. This journey helped me grow. Even though I thought it was one of my lowest moments it was a defining moment in a series of events that would frame my future.

The second loss was different for me. This time I blamed God. How can I be such a good person, faithful, loyal, a tither, and still lose my baby? I stopped praying. I stopped reading my bible and I became sad. Sad every time my cycle came. Sad every time I had to buy sanitary napkins and sad when two of my best friends were pregnant at the same time and I was not. Thank God there was a turning point!

Two things happened that helped us move forward in our fertility journey. I was given a book called Supernatural Childbirth by Jackie Mize, from someone at my church and I began to read it and say the prayers in the book. We also had the opportunity to get help and even though I knew we would soon have some answers I was still reluctant. **I didn't want to be disappointed again.** Why get my hopes up to be let down? With some anxiety we went to the infertility specialist and found out that I had an adhesion in my uterus that may have been the cause of the miscarriages! An adhesion is scar tissue that was in my uterus. If the baby is attached to this adhesion it would not receive the adequate blood supply needed for growth and would result in a loss. This, surprisingly, was a moment of relief. Finding out that we could soon try again was a blessing, but I had to have surgery to remove the adhesion.

After successful removal of the adhesion, we became pregnant! One year later we had our son Garth Jr. without any in-vitro services. I know you

MEMOIRS OF ALMOST BARREN WOMEN:
OUR JOURNEY TO MOTHERHOOD

---

may be thinking, "This seems like an easy process for her." It was not. My marriage suffered, my faith suffered, and I didn't share any of my emotions fully with my spouse.

I am writing this testimony to encourage you. **It is not your fault.** You are of great value to Christ and your desires are of great importance to Him. I learned during this process that I was selfish and a bit prideful. These traumatic events, while bringing revelation also brought me closer to my husband and closer to Christ.

I've learned the importance of being your own advocate. Do research about miscarriages and infertility on your own so that you can make the choices that are best for your situation. I've come to the realization that every pregnancy is a miracle whether we prepare for the child or not.

Being a woman of color in a society where we don't talk much about our vulnerabilities, I want to let you know that it is okay to be vulnerable. It's okay to grieve over your loss or losses and its okay to get help. I know that you are strong but even a strong woman needs someone to lift her burdens when she cannot. Let your journey be something that you LIVE through. Do not let it make you bitter. You will come out of this better than you can imagine.

Geneva

CHAPTER 03

Challenges

MEMOIRS OF ALMOST BARREN WOMEN:
OUR JOURNEY TO MOTHERHOOD

> We encounter many defeats, but we must not be defeated!
>
> **MAYA ANGELOU**

Infertility causes run the gamut. Some people have one cause, some have multiple, and then some have no clearly defined reason to explain their inability to conceive.

Which one might be better I ask? I boldly declare none of the above. Any adult who wishes to conceive would weigh their fertility issues at a 1000 out of 10.

The diagnosis is dreadful. I recall our first day at the fertility specialist. The doctor automatically assumed I was young, healthy, viable, and because I was pregnant before it had to be my husband. He immediately ran down several reasons it was likely him. It was awkward, demeaning, and presumptuous to say the least.

However, he was a professional, an expert and he had to know right? No. He was wrong. After sperm analysis, lab work, and a couple visits. My husband had a lofty, viable, sperm count and no factors contributing to why we had not gotten pregnant.

My previously concerned husband. Who thought, "Well I have never gotten anyone pregnant, maybe he is right" could now breathe a sigh of relief. He was not a contributory factor in our lack of conception.

MEMOIRS OF ALMOST BARREN WOMEN:
OUR JOURNEY TO MOTHERHOOD

Well, who's left? Me, that's who, with a big old target on my forehead. It left me wondering what was wrong with me. Can this be fixed or is it permanent? Does my husband blame me? What's next? Questions, doubts, and fears ran the gamut. The doctor never apologized to my husband for his prejudgment, instead he just moved on.

In the United States, 10% to 15% of couples are infertile (MayoClinic.org, 2020). It can be related to either the male or female reproductive system. It can be one or both. One of the biggest challenges can be the lack of symptoms. Meanwhile, some women and men can trace their fertility issues back through a trail of medical problems; many have little to no related health problems.

Challenge # 1   **How can one fix what they are not aware of?**

> Sometimes the best you can do is not think, not wonder, not imagine, not obsess, just breathe and have faith that everything will work out for the best.
>
> **UNKNOWN**

Other challenges include, but are not limited to, age, abnormal menstrual cycles, ovulation disorders, infections, endometriosis, sexually transmitted diseases, cancer treatments, muscular dystrophy, low sperm count, testicular or prostate problems, blocked or scarred fallopian tubes, hysterectomy, poor sperm movement, abnormal sperm shape and/or family history reproductive problems.

MEMOIRS OF ALMOST BARREN WOMEN:
OUR JOURNEY TO MOTHERHOOD

But perhaps the biggest challenges are moving on, giving up, being at peace with your reality, using alternative methods to become a parent, and/or embracing others as they celebrate their new babies.

I toggle back and forth with being okay with not being able to bear children unassisted. I tell myself and others, "I am okay with having one, but I would not have been okay with none." I also used to feel good that "my issue" was quickly remedied once I sought help.

However, I don't think it's 100% true. Every month I hope I miss my period and get to be surprised that I am pregnant. I imagine surprising my husband and son with the news. I wish "my issue" was prayed away, but it was not and even though I was successful with one round of infertility treatment, the decision and process are never easy. Instead, it is a complicated reality that can lead to a cluster of other trials, barriers, and stress.

Many times, I have planned out in my head how I would keep it secret from others for as long as possible to avoid having to share my disappointment should something unfortunate were to happen. Sadly, preparing for dread instead of believing for the best.

For this reason, I know I am grateful for my one blessing, but deep down I wish and pray for more. I pray for my husband to get on board because I want him to have the same desires that I have. I want him to be engaged, excited, and participate. For now, he is over it and has accepted our only child as our destiny, but I have not.

MEMOIRS OF ALMOST BARREN WOMEN:
OUR JOURNEY TO MOTHERHOOD

I hold on to the hope my first fertility specialist gave me that I could become pregnant on my own. My diagnosis at the time did not deem me 100% infertile. However, almost ten years later no unassisted pregnancies have occurred.

I have to accept it and move on and someday I will.

MEMOIRS OF ALMOST BARREN WOMEN:
OUR JOURNEY TO MOTHERHOOD

Nicole's Journey

> I was angry at myself and at my body.

CHAPTER - 03

MEMOIRS OF ALMOST BARREN WOMEN:
OUR JOURNEY TO MOTHERHOOD

Having children was not something I ever really thought about. I figured when I was ready it would just happen. I met my husband, Chris, in 2004 and we married in 2009 when I was 28. We knew we wanted children, so about six months after being married we officially began trying. I knew it could take a few months for it to happen, so I wasn't overly concerned when we weren't pregnant right away. Disappointed but not concerned.

Unfortunately, month after month passed and nothing. When we reached the one-year mark of trying I decided to speak with my gynecologist. She suggested, as I was almost thirty, to see a fertility specialist so we made an appointment. That first appointment was overwhelming, to say the least. We left with a lot of information and a list of procedures I would need to have to make sure everything was working as it should.

During this testing we found that I had adhesions in and around my fallopian tubes and my ovaries. Essentially, my fallopian tubes were blocked. My heart was crushed. I felt like my body had failed me. What had I done to my body to cause this? Surgery was recommended to try and remove the adhesions and see if my fallopian tubes were salvageable.

According to my doctor the adhesions were so thick it took her over an hour to clean them out but thankfully I was able to keep my tubes. After surgery, we decided to try on our own without medical intervention. The doctor will follow my ovulation and let us know when to try. A few months of this and nothing. No pregnancy. The stress of this process was taking a toll on our marriage. It felt like we were putting too much pressure on ourselves and it was causing conflict between us. We prayed about it and decided to take a break.

MEMOIRS OF ALMOST BARREN WOMEN:
OUR JOURNEY TO MOTHERHOOD

In September of 2012, during our "break" I found out I was pregnant. We were so happy! God did it! Our dream of becoming parents had come true! I immediately went back to the fertility specialist so my numbers could be monitored, and we could make sure everything was progressing as it should.

Unfortunately, our joy did not last. The pregnancy was ectopic. The doctor had told us with the history of my tubes an ectopic is common. I was given an injection that basically ended the pregnancy. To say I was devastated would be an understatement. My heart was broken. I felt broken. I left that doctors office feeling lost and heartbroken.

Thereafter, it was recommended that we try in vitro fertilization or IVF. We did not have any insurance coverage or financial means at that time to pay out of pocket, so it was not an option for us. We decided to go ahead and get a second opinion. During the process of our second opinion, it was found that my adhesions had grown back on my tubes and ovaries and I was also diagnosed with polycystic ovarian syndrome or PCOS. Our second opinion ultimately resulted in the same recommendation of IVF.

I was angry at myself and at my body. How could it not do the one thing God had created it to do? What had I done to my body to cause this? I did not live the best life prior to becoming saved. Was all this my fault? My faith refused to let me believe that I would not have a child. God called us to be fruitful and multiply. Who was I to question God's word?

We decided to put fertility treatments on hold and save for IVF all the while praying that God would still give us a child naturally. It was not an easy decision. I wanted immediate results. I won't lie and say my faith

MEMOIRS OF ALMOST BARREN WOMEN:
OUR JOURNEY TO MOTHERHOOD

did not falter during this time. Thankfully, I have a husband who is grounded in faith and refuses to let me fall. In July 2014, at 32, **I found out I was pregnant again**, naturally! I couldn't believe it, two years of negative tests and heartbreak and here I was holding a positive test! But God! I was nervous that this would be another ectopic, so I went back to the fertility specialist. I closely monitored and praised God this pregnancy had made it to the uterus. There was a gestational sac! I just knew this was it.

Sadly, at about six weeks my levels began dropping and nothing developed inside the sac. I had to have a D & C (dilation and curettage) to have the tissue from this pregnancy loss removed. I remember going home from the hospital and lying in bed crying. I couldn't understand why this was happening again. During this time my husband got a job with insurance that covered IVF. We thought this must definitely be a sign that IVF was the route we should go. My brain said this, but my heart never followed along. My spirit never felt IVF was our journey, so I hesitated. We agreed to wait a little longer and keep praying about what we should do.

In June 2015 I found out I was pregnant again, naturally! I will be honest and say that I did not immediately feel joy. I was fearful. Would this be the one or would I be heading down another miscarriage journey? The pregnancy started great, numbers were rising wonderfully, and there was a gestational sac. At six and half weeks I saw and heard my baby's heartbeat. I cannot explain the joy that spread through me. This was the furthest we'd ever progressed, and I just knew this was it! At eight weeks I went in for my weekly ultrasound to monitor the growth and learned that my baby's heartbeat had stopped at seven weeks and two days. I couldn't grasp this news. **Why?** What has gone wrong? I'd just heard the heartbeat strong and steady 1 week ago. I could see the pain on my husband's face. But he held me strong because I fell apart.

MEMOIRS OF ALMOST BARREN WOMEN:
OUR JOURNEY TO MOTHERHOOD

Fast forward, we were able to do genetic testing on this pregnancy and found that our baby had an extra X chromosome, XXY, therefore likely would not have lived a normal healthy life. I hold tight to the fact that he is in heaven healthy and strong.

The time after this loss and diagnosis was not a good one for me. I was so angry and hurt and I took it out on God. I wanted my baby. I told my husband that he should leave me and that he deserved a wife who wasn't broken and could give him the children he wanted. I thank God for a husband who loved me unconditionally during this time and held me up spiritually when I couldn't move past my grief and anger. We decided at this point to hold off on IVF or even trying naturally. I needed to get my spirit right again. I found solace in the song "Silence" by Anthony Evans and the scripture 1 Samuel 1:27-28. I also began reading Supernatural Childbirth by Jackie Mize. These things really helped to restore my faith.

Every January our church does a voluntary fast. During this fast I prayed to God that he would reveal his plan for our fertility journey. Not long after this fast started, we were approached by a family member about fostering to adopt a baby girl. I immediately wanted to say yes, I'd always wanted to foster but my husband was more hesitant. He had always wanted biological children first. He prayed about it and agreed. We met Aaliyah when she was two weeks old. The moment I held her in my arms I knew that she was meant to be mine.

Immediately we started classes to become foster parent certified. Aaliyah was officially placed with us on Aug 29, 2017 at seven months old. My heart was full of joy. I loved this child so much. On January 1st, 2018 we got a call asking us if we'd be willing to take her sibling that had just been

MEMOIRS OF ALMOST BARREN WOMEN:
OUR JOURNEY TO MOTHERHOOD

born. I knew I couldn't say no. She came home the next day. We went from no children to two children in the span of four months. It was overwhelming and hard at first. We had some struggles, but we made it. Not long after Jada was born, at one of our court hearings, the judge agreed to start a reunification plan with their shared birth father. He had not been in the picture until now.

The next year and a half were filled with a lot of ups and downs with this process. There were multiple times when I thought we were going to lose our girls, **my children** who I loved more than I could ever imagine. Then, in July 2018 I found out I was pregnant again. What a surprise. Will I call it a joyful surprise? No, I wouldn't. I felt guilty. I'd always wanted to have a biological child but now with two small children? Would I be able to do this? Unfortunately, we found out this pregnancy was also ectopic. I had to have surgery and due to the size and placement of the embryo I lost my right fallopian tube. And was told that my left tube was in pretty bad shape. At this point I had had it. I was angry as to why this kept happening and I was heartbroken. I told my husband that I could not do this anymore, my heart cannot handle any more loss. He agreed.

Shortly after my last pregnancy my girls' biological father decided that the best thing for the girls was to remain with us. So, on August 16, 2019 we were able to adopt Aaliyah and Jada. I could barely get the words out in court because I was crying so hard. These beautiful girls who came into my life when I least expected it, healed me, and were officially mine.

I realized that all this time I had been praying for my children to come from my body but that was not God's plan. When I finally asked God to show me his plan, not my plan, He did. I was selfish in thinking my way was the only way. God's plan is not always what we think it should be nor

MEMOIRS OF ALMOST BARREN WOMEN:
OUR JOURNEY TO MOTHERHOOD

will it happen when we want it to. But we must trust in His word that never fails. Was the foster care and adoption journey easy? No. It was frustrating, heartbreaking and hard but I wouldn't trade it for anything. It gave me the children of my heart. These children were meant to be ours. Is our journey over? Only God knows. I will follow whatever road He leads us down.

Nicole

CHAPTER 04

Who Suffers from Infertility?

MEMOIRS OF ALMOST BARREN WOMEN:
OUR JOURNEY TO MOTHERHOOD

> Realize that you are not alone, that we are in this together and most importantly that there is hope.
>
> **DEEPIKA PADUKONE**

Although it is commonly assumed women are predominantly responsible for infertility issues, Brennan Peterson of the Washington Post cites both the U.S. Department of Health and Human Services and the National Institute of Health who account for one-third of the cases being male related, one-third being attributed to the female partner, and one third being a combination of factors from the male and female (2018). He adds this misconception as a myth trailing back as far as stories in the bible.

In my personal life, and then later in my research I was astonished to learn how many families were quietly suffering through this alone. It bothered me that women and men were living in shame thinking they were the outlier. According to Fertility Health, only two percentage points separate male and female infertility rates in the United States (Genesis Fertility & Reproductive Medicine, 2019). In fact, the impact is greater than most people know.

Infertility affects at least 12% of all women up to age 44, and research suggests black women are twice as likely to experience infertility as white women. Yet only 8% of Black women between the ages of 25-44 seek medical help to get pregnant, compared to 15% of white women (Fertility for Colored Girls, 2020).

MEMOIRS OF ALMOST BARREN WOMEN:
OUR JOURNEY TO MOTHERHOOD

I have read articles that indicate that one in ten women are affected by infertility. That is profound. It is also the reason we need more books written, more stories shared, more legislation passed, more medical benefits, and more awareness to support one another during this plight.

Just imagine one in ten women. That means in any given setting in any given room, a woman within 100 feet of you is experiencing this simultaneously with you. You are not alone.

When I was younger, this was something that was never talked about. I cannot even recall a woman that I knew that openly shared fertility issues or was receiving care for fertility treatment.

However, I now know of many more women who have suffered stillbirths, miscarriages, and infertility struggles. I am aware of many families who seek or have sought infertility care. Even in writing this book and looking for contributors and editors' women have disclosed that they too are unwanted members of this club. It is a club where the membership is costly. The fee is astronomical, and participation is involuntary.

In a 2017 article, nearly 232,000 IVF cycles were completed in 2015, which was up 68% from 2006 according to the Centers for Disease Control and Prevention (Carnes, 2017).

Unfortunately, it is still faux pas. There is still shame and embarrassment and this is limiting and, in some cases, crippling. When we avoid sharing, we do not get the support we need, and we are unable to support others going through the same trials. Instead, we muffle our screams, we mask our pain, and we put on a brave face in public, but when in private or alone we are left with our own anguish, loneliness, self-pity, or grief.

MEMOIRS OF ALMOST BARREN WOMEN:
OUR JOURNEY TO MOTHERHOOD

When we have partners involved, it affects them as well. This includes some of our other intimate relationships. In a Washington Post article, Peterson shares, "a diagnosis can alter relationships, lead to depression and anxiety, and threaten lifelong expectations of parenthood (Five Myths about Infertility, 2018)."

If you are one of the undesirable members of this horrid club, I support you and your efforts along the way. Unlike the joys of a planned pregnancy, these visits are often unhappy and definitely not exciting. This journey is not one of paradise, but the roads are winding, bumpy, and the raw truth is sometimes it may lead to a dead end.

What we can hold on to is our options and our hope. It doesn't have to be a dream, it can be a reality, but it will mean being flexible, patient, and open to options.

Whatever the path, I support you and you are not alone. Knowing the struggle, I pray for even those I do not know who have to navigate through this.

MEMOIRS OF ALMOST BARREN WOMEN:
OUR JOURNEY TO MOTHERHOOD

Robin's Journey

> If you are going through this process you have to be determined because you will be told more about the negative outcomes than the positive outcomes.

MEMOIRS OF ALMOST BARREN WOMEN:
OUR JOURNEY TO MOTHERHOOD

This morning when I woke up I had four legs coming from my head and six arms from my feet and more heads than I went to bed with. I obviously had difficulty moving but I managed to get up and start breakfast for my family of five.

I'm in the kitchen now starting my day as a short order cook. Each of my children are very different and very beautiful little people. My son is now 8 years old and marks the start of my journey.

My husband and I got married on September 29, 2007. We were full of dreams, so many dreams. My husband was pursuing music in ministry. He started teaching music and piano at a private school and quickly began to realize his dream moving toward ministry. I received several promotions on my job and we were in a good place. We just knew at any moment things would change for us and we would be announcing the birth of our first child.

The plan was to have at least two children. From the moment we got married, on our honeymoon, the plan was to get pregnant. I really thought it would be that simple. I never considered that there would be any struggle getting pregnant until after the first year of our marriage. Even though I was approaching 40 my initial thought was to review all the home remedies and web solutions. Yes, we tried all of the right positions and more. We purchased the kits and kept dates and times but with no results. **Each time, I thought this is it**. This month will be the month.

Another year went by and it became serious. I found myself at the fertility clinic. Wow. There were signs that I had completely ignored. I knew I had fibroid tumors, but I read from "Dr. Internet" that they would shrink during pregnancy. I didn't realize that mine had grown significantly large

MEMOIRS OF ALMOST BARREN WOMEN:
OUR JOURNEY TO MOTHERHOOD

preventing pregnancy and perhaps the collapse of one of my fallopian tubes. The fibroid tumors would have to be removed. At this point, so much time had elapsed the doctor was recommending that we immediately consider in vitro fertilization (IVF). There were other options but with me quickly approaching 40 there was no time to waste.

    I have to take a moment and let you know that at this time I had no fear. It just felt like a process we would just have to walk out. I had a lot to learn about the process, but I was ready. Let's get this done. This feeling of determination was routed in the Word of God. If you are going through this process you have to be determined because you will be told more about the negative outcomes than the positive outcomes. While doctors do have success, I think people tend to cover themselves by presenting the probability of the negative. You will hear there is a 10% chance that this won't happen versus hearing there is a 90% chance that you will have success. So, don't rely on the confidence of the doctor or those around you. Rely solely on the Word of God and what God has for you.

    After three transfers of five eggs and two pregnancies. I was so confident that we had overcome this hurdle. We had so many great prayer warriors praying around us reminding us of God's promises. We knew that God's plan was for us to have children. So, when we lost this one it was heart breaking. **Why wasn't my faith sufficient?** I think that was harder to get over than the loss of the baby and I was exhausted. I was convinced that it was God's will for me to have children, but I had no desire to go through the process again. Lying in bed next to my husband adoption dropped into my spirit. I looked over at my husband and asked, "What do you think about adoption?" He looked at me and said, "I was going to ask you the same thing."

MEMOIRS OF ALMOST BARREN WOMEN:
OUR JOURNEY TO MOTHERHOOD

God's plan for us did not change but His path was not what I had expected. The Word tells us that God's ways is not our way. I have seen this repeated in my life many times in other areas, but I had a very narrow focus when it came to having children.

My faith began to strengthen but my body was very weak. I have been through so much both physically and emotionally. I really felt like I was running on fumes. Just going through the motions. We finally decided on an agency that we wanted to go with and after doing some of the initial group meetings we decided to complete the online application. I remember as I completed the adoption application that my mind was so foggy that I didn't submit the application that evening and when I woke the next day, I just looked at it and closed my laptop. I couldn't hit submit.

The next day while on my way into the office, I called my husband and asked him if he was sure. He reassured me that we were moving in the right direction, but we decided to wait. "We will just pray and if we have peace in the morning, we will submit the application then." I loved him for that. It was such a weight off my shoulder. I went to work and didn't really think about it again until I was leaving the office.

Later, I was still physically tired as I was driving to a meeting. A friend called and asked me to pick her up so that we could go to the meeting together. Our friend was fostering a baby that could potentially be available for adoption. We did go on to adopt that precious little baby. I fell in love with him the moment I saw him.

While I moved quickly through this story and sometimes it seems like everything happened just that fast; nothing was that immediate. It was all connected. God had a perfect plan for me, and I needed to navigate down

MEMOIRS OF ALMOST BARREN WOMEN:
OUR JOURNEY TO MOTHERHOOD

that particular path to get me to the position he needed me to be in. Down to the very end where I was too exhausted to make proactive decisions on my own which I would typically do.

During this time, I prayed often but my challenge has always been the waiting. I pray and then move. And while there is a place for that, there is a time to pray and wait. It's definitely not my forte but I am confident that God knows what's best for me and He knows exactly how to move me out of my own way. I never stopped trusting Him.

God answered our prayers through adoption in a way that I cannot put into words. I prayed daily for our son way before the adoption was final, way before we even met him. We would pray for us to be matched with not the perfect child but a child that we could effectively parent with a personality comparable to our own. We prayed for his health

We prayed for his happiness. We prayed not for a perfect child but for a child perfect for us.

We continued to grow our family through adoption. We have three children and each of our children were handpicked for us by God and because of that we are blessed, we are whole, and we are complete.

The Word of God says to trust in the Lord with all your heart and lean not to your own understanding. In all your ways acknowledge Him and He will direct your path (Prov. 3:5-6). Know that God has a plan, and that plan includes children. He loves children more than you do and it is His gift to you (Ps. 127:3).

CHAPTER 05

Infertility and Me

MEMOIRS OF ALMOST BARREN WOMEN:
OUR JOURNEY TO MOTHERHOOD

> Sometimes it's the smallest decisions that can change your life forever.
>
> **KERI RUSSELL**

My oldest memory of a younger me......

I remember having a glass tea set and having tea and biscuits with my paternal grandmother. That memory competes with the memory of me climbing the cabinets in Cherry Bay, Florida to get food while my mom lay asleep in the next room. I think I was either making a mayonnaise or peanut butter and jelly sandwich.

Although I shudder at the thought of eating a mayonnaise sandwich now, my memory of eating them back then is not only comforting, I remember enjoying them. I am unsure which of the two memories precedes the other.

When I think of the woman I am now those memories make perfect sense of the shape of me. The woman I was to become. The resilience I obtained and the ability to get it done with little or with abundance. When faced with challenges I celebrate my humble experiences. Challenges I know I can sustain, due to the triumphs of past experiences and humble beginnings.

Oftentimes people resent their past because of things like living in poverty, struggling, or growing up in undesirable circumstances. However, our past shapes us. It shapes our actions and behaviors. It shapes our fears and our thoughts and unfortunately it can shape our health, our decision making, and outlook on life.

MEMOIRS OF ALMOST BARREN WOMEN:
OUR JOURNEY TO MOTHERHOOD

You may be wondering what this has to do with my fertility. Well let's connect the dots. I strongly believe everything is related and manifested out of something else in your life.

For example, my lack of trust came from me witnessing many models of broken relationships from childhood to early adulthood. After witnessing family and friends being mistreated, neglected, abused, and used by men, I created what I believed was a way to avoid those circumstances happening to me.

In my early dating life, I would be mean and aggressive to suitors. I would be evasive and limited my vulnerability in relationships. I would end a relationship with any sign of mistrust, lies, or lack of support. I took "I can do bad all by myself" to a whole other level. I thought if I leave them before they leave me, I cannot be hurt or at least limit the damage. If I don't commit, I can't be cheated on, or if I focus on me, I won't get lost in them, it was these things and more.

Don't let me lose you, I am getting there. What I saw growing up shaped how I felt about relationships and it affected how I interacted with them. I lacked trust and wanted to prioritize my needs, feelings, and desires. In relation to this I would say, "I am not going to be a baby mama." I also declared I wouldn't be in a relationship with someone whose values didn't mirror mine, and I would not have kids before I could provide for them without living check to check.

I'm almost there. Stay with me. What I should have declared and lived out was avoiding premarital sex and/or unprotected sex. What I should have declared was being more discretionary and protective of my reproductive

MEMOIRS OF ALMOST BARREN WOMEN:
OUR JOURNEY TO MOTHERHOOD

health and body. And I should not have chosen to be in sexual relationships with men who didn't value me, respect me, and protect me!

Instead, I focused on temporary emotions and my financial future. Those were the drivers of my decisions when I engaged in unprotected premarital sex on two separate occasions. Once at age 17 and then again at the age of 21. I was in a relationship with guys who paid me a lot of attention but were not connected to my destiny. My temporary need to have companionship led to me engaging in sex and subsequently getting pregnant in both instances.

As you may recall, I was adamant about not getting played, not being stuck as a single mother, and not being financially unstable, this drove my decision to decide to abort both pregnancies.

Abortion should not be a form of birth control; however, this is how I utilized it. I wanted a particular lifestyle and instead of being proactive and making decisions to facilitate this desired lifestyle I was reactive and chose to make a less acceptable choice. I hope you didn't miss the connection. The poor relationships I witnessed lead to personal defense mechanisms, and it influenced poor choices.

In turn, I remember getting sick after each abortion. With the first one, I don't know to this day if it was a dream or reality, but I have a memory of waking during the procedure. I could see the staff working and then remember drifting back off. After the procedure I remember being asked to sit up in a chair and also to go to the bathroom. I believe these two things help to determine if I was safe enough to be discharged home.

MEMOIRS OF ALMOST BARREN WOMEN:
OUR JOURNEY TO MOTHERHOOD

After getting home I was extremely nauseous, drowsy, and in pain. So, I slept and slept and slept. I couldn't eat and didn't want to do anything.

At some point I remember getting up and trying to eat but was unsuccessful. I tried to go to the bathroom, but needed assistance, I was weak and still in pain. During this time, I started to become feverish, have chills, and feel like I had lock jaw. I couldn't chew, my jaw line was stiff, and I was extremely restless.

I don't remember if I was taking the medication, but I believe I was in some form of septic shock after the procedure. It is only by God's grace I am here and then somehow the antibiotics and my immune system eventually resolved these symptoms and this was not a fatal story.

If I had to guess either I had a botched procedure, a complication from the procedure, or just a weird reaction to the medications or anesthesia used. I have no way of substantiating any of those hypotheses, but something happened and that something I believed affected my reproductive system as well.

To give you a little more background. I remember dating a guy who I didn't particularly want to be with and was not attracted to, but he pursued and pursued until I gave in. It was a very insignificant relationship to say the least, but he had the title of being my boyfriend at the age of 17.

After several encounters of unprotected sex, I became pregnant. It was no doubt in my mind at that time. I was not prepared to be a mother; he was totally unfit to be a dad. Not to mention he went to jail shortly after I disclosed, I was pregnant, and I already knew what I was going to do. I'd

MEMOIRS OF ALMOST BARREN WOMEN:
OUR JOURNEY TO MOTHERHOOD

often wreck my brain about this and riddle myself with guilt, because prior to getting pregnant I knew I was unprepared for motherhood and all that it would bring.

There I was, 17 years old, in the 12th grade pregnant with a "baby daddy" in jail. I was a baby mama, even if it was only for a few weeks. Not only did I let myself down, but I also cowardly let my mom down as well. You see, she was very open with me, she trusted me, and we had several conversations about sex. She kept the door open for discussions about sex, boys, and protection. Yet I made my own path to destruction.

Then there was the second one. I failed to take the antibiotics because I didn't have them and the "boyfriend" I had decided on the day of the scheduled procedure that he would not go with me to have the procedure. At the last minute I had to call for help. I had to call a friends' mom because no one else knew and I wanted to keep it that way. She didn't have a car, so I picked her up and she took me to the clinic. Afterwards, I was sleepy from the sedation and pain medications, so she dropped me off and kept my car.

I slept the rest of the day and most of the next day at home alone. Powering through yet another challenge I would face alone but was determined to come out stronger on the other side. Fast forward 48 hours after the procedure I began to develop fever and chills again. It wasn't until then I acknowledged, I didn't pick up my medication and start my prescribed antibiotics. I had developed an infection.

I called this so-called boyfriend and he downplayed my concerns and symptoms, and again left me hanging with no support. He did not come to my aid and I had to figure out a way to get the antibiotics. I called this friend

MEMOIRS OF ALMOST BARREN WOMEN:
OUR JOURNEY TO MOTHERHOOD

again and thank God she was still there for me. She picked up the pills and some other things and brought them to me.

However, what I realize now the damage was already done. My infection led to scarring and blocking my fallopian tubes. The passageway for sperm to get to the egg to impregnate them. Life as I knew it had changed, but I was ignorant to it all. I was "almost barren" and had no clue.

I will share more details later, but in short, I am one of the women who blames herself, blames my choices, and realized too late my lack of knowledge and awareness surrounding reproductive health and wellness contributed to that.

My transparency is not to upset pro-lifers or those trying to get pregnant by callously sharing my choice to have two abortions. Instead, I hope young ladies and women who read this use this as awareness of the potential consequences of aborting. I want to empower others to be proactive instead of reactive.

Please note: many women/families do not play a part in their infertility, but those of us who do with the right knowledge and awareness we can be equipped to avoid these pitfalls to anguish and bareness.

Long story short, I was smart enough not to become a baby mom, however, not smart enough to avoid having premarital sex. In addition, I wasn't smart enough not to have unprotected sexual experiences.

MEMOIRS OF ALMOST BARREN WOMEN:
OUR JOURNEY TO MOTHERHOOD

Let's wrap up the second not-so-proud moment. I had an on-again-off-again relationship with a man who put me down and kept me a secret. He was the one and only man to ever make me doubt my worth. You see he pursued me and pursued me until I gave in. The unrelenting efforts coupled with the help of one of my older cousins who said, "You see all those pretty girls with ugly guys, but they have everything, you better get with him!" So, there I was, young, single, and worn down in his pursuit, I gave the relationship a try. He was in my judgment hard to look at, so initially I didn't want to be seen with him.

Fast forward several months to some years later I didn't understand why he never took me anywhere, had never introduced me to his family, and did more for others than he did for me. Yet, I continued this unhealthy relationship where I continued to have sex with him, all the while being talked down to and played over and over again.

I recall early in the relationship he would often promise that if I went back to school, he would help me. It never happened. I began nursing school, I struggled to pay bills, maintain a used vehicle, and cover college costs. Often, I would beg for his help. Sometimes he would flat out say no, other times he would lie and not come through, or provide a portion of what he agreed to. There was a period of time when my bills were overdue, and I would come home on my lunch break and beg for his help. Only for him to refuse to assist me. I would cry myself through my lunch breaks, pull my big girl panties up and return to work.

Where was this love for self then I wondered? Where was this love of God? I was looking to him when I was living unholy and not putting my trust in God. I thought he was my source with his drug money, of which he

MEMOIRS OF ALMOST BARREN WOMEN:
OUR JOURNEY TO MOTHERHOOD

had plenty, he could have easily made the journey easier. Despite over two years of this unproductive, unsupportive relationship, I continued to have unprotected sex with this man, and which left me at 21 pregnant again with a baby I was not prepared to care for.

You read that right, I was pregnant again just 4 years later and still had no desire to be a baby mama. With no one to blame but myself, I was with a man who could not walk with me into my destiny. So, I decided to abort yet another baby. I was playing God again. I knew the man I was giving my body to did not respect or honor me. Nor did he treat me in a way I deserved. In addition, he was a devout Muslim and I was a Christian. Despite my actions, I knew I could never deny Jesus and take up the Muslim faith.

The man who got me pregnant never respected me. I have to admit, I was used. I was something to do. In part, I was doing the same with him. It was a dysfunctional relationship of convenience. There were two instances I would dare to say he raped me or at the very least took advantage of me. Once in my apartment I had taken two Benadryl prior to him coming over. I could barely keep my eyes open and lay there partially sedated but refusing sex. I recall being extremely sleepy and drowsy. He didn't care, he wanted sex and would proceed with intercourse without my participation.

In a later instance, I thought I was stopping by his house with the intent to get money, when he forced me onto an empty mattress, and we wrestled around as he ripped my panties off again forcing himself on me and proceeding to have sex without my consent and would proceed with intercourse without my participation. I remember saying in my head afterwards, "he raped me." I rationalized that he was a guy companion of mine and I didn't scream or cry. I just lay there despite not wanting to have sex. Did that make it consensual?

MEMOIRS OF ALMOST BARREN WOMEN:
OUR JOURNEY TO MOTHERHOOD

Should I have done more to stop him? Should I hate him?

I finally decided after this same man asked me, "How come you never asked or told me to stop selling drugs?" I didn't have an answer then, nor do I have one now. I do, however, feel like he was another man, wanting to be validated by someone else. Waiting for a particular woman to help him before he would embark on a better life. I knew I was not his gateway. I wanted a man with a plan and a dream that would go on with or without me. After deciding to no longer date this type of guy and focus on myself, I finally ended that relationship and decided I would be alone. I realized that even though the lifestyle was fun, it had its limitations and I would never be satisfied.

For years I resented him. I felt like I gave myself to someone who took me for granted and discarded my feelings and did not acknowledge my worth. I blamed him for not being there, helping to take away what was so precious, and my ability to bear children. I often wanted to tell him, but I didn't

Now I own my part and my individual decisions, and I am grateful to God for alternatives to bringing life into the world. Some time passed and I was focused with no distractions. Work, school, church, and family. Hanging out here and there with no expectations. Then my friend became my boyfriend. Within 10 months he proposed. I finished nursing school and we began to plan a wedding. Just under 200 people and the biggest celebration of my life. We decided about 4 years into the marriage to try for a baby. During marriage counseling we agreed on two babies.

This would soon prove to be more difficult than we would have known.

MEMOIRS OF ALMOST BARREN WOMEN:
OUR JOURNEY TO MOTHERHOOD

For three years we would had sex without birth control and I never became pregnant. After some time, we agreed to see a fertility specialist. Prior to going, I was confident it had little to do with me. After all, I was already pregnant twice before. During the 1st consult, the provider went on to inform my husband it was likely an issue on his side as well. He pointed out that my husband was in his late 20's and never had any babies. After several test and sperm counts. No issues were found.

The plan was to check in with me next. I go to a series of visits, ultrasounds, and a painful test where they would shoot dye through my fallopian tubes to check for their patency. Then the answers start to come.

Like many African American women, I had cysts, but more than that I had Polycystic Ovarian Syndrome also known as PCOS. The news of this coupled with finding out that one of my tubes was completely blocked and the other was partially blocked. To me it was devastating news. The doctor seemed unfazed and he would go on to reassure me that I would be able to get pregnant and could do so naturally if I decided to wait. However, at this point I yearned to have a baby and didn't want to wait any longer.

We agreed to start the fertility process. The treatment plan would include surgically removing the cysts and taking pills that would cause me to go through a phase that would mimic menopause. Afterward Che would provide sperm, they would retrieve eggs from me, fertilize them with the sperm and implant them in me. It was an emotionally trying time. Not many people knew and I was embarrassed. I also blamed myself tremendously.

MEMOIRS OF ALMOST BARREN WOMEN:
OUR JOURNEY TO MOTHERHOOD

Had it not been for me to play God with my two abortions, maybe I wouldn't be in this predicament. Recalling after each abortion I got sick. It was the after effects of these two miscarriages that I believe contributed solely to my infertility. I secretly blamed myself for my wonderful husband being with a barren woman. It was my fault this deserving man, decided to marry a woman with a casual and immature past that resulted in my inability to conceive children naturally. Despite the circumstances he never blamed me. He just loved and supported me.

After countless pills, injections, and doctors' visits it was here. It was the big day. I was anxious. We were scrubbed up and in the waiting area. Today would be the day they implanted my fertilized embryos. We had previously decided they would implant two. Despite this previous agreement as they wheeled me into the operating room, the doctor stopped just shy of the operating room (OR) door to recommend they implant three embryos to ensure a successful procedure. He explained my options. One of the options being selective reduction, where I could abort one or two babies to ensure I only had one pregnancy.

I remember wondering, how could he do this? My stress level was already at an all-time high and I didn't have time to think it through or discuss it with my husband. Also, how could I abort another baby? Especially after all I went through. If I was given an opportunity to have another child, or children I would never abort another baby. I was done playing God. I finally realized the gift of life was not mine to decide or deny. We stayed with the original plan, and only implanted two.

Fast forward a few weeks later and the pregnancy test was finally positive. I had taken many in the past with first sight of nausea, or even being

MEMOIRS OF ALMOST BARREN WOMEN:
OUR JOURNEY TO MOTHERHOOD

a day late with my period. I had longed to be called mommy. My husband had previously decided that if God wanted us to conceive a child it would happen otherwise, we should accept it and move on. I would repeat till this day that I would be happy with one, but totally unhappy with none. That was one of my roles as a woman, right? Be fruitful and multiply. It was an expectation of a wife to grow and nurture the family wasn't it? At least in my mind it was, and for that I was sadden, felt guilty, and blamed myself and my choices.

I often wondered if my husband was 100% honest. Could he really be satisfied with having no children? No one to call his namesake? No one to teach about life. Could he really be satisfied without having teeny, little eyes that looked like him? He was in fact against adoption and fostering a kid. I would have totally done it.

Thanks, be unto God, I would never know. On July 31st, 2011 after 12 hours of labor and an episiotomy God showed his mercy and granted us the most beautiful big-headed little boy on earth. Che Baye' Willis Jr. was born. Healthy and strong weighing 7 lbs. 11 oz. and 21 inches long.

Thinking back, I enjoyed everything about him. I was super appreciative to God that I waited to raise him. I had the knowledge and wisdom to raise and parent him. I would report all of our 1st to my sister, who was also expecting and whomever else would listen. I wasn't the only one excited and Godly proud. My husband was really protective of him, attentive to his needs and although he won't admit it, he was competing with me for bonding time. Although I was breastfeeding, he would often rush to get the frozen breastmilk and feed him via bottle. My husband would also talk to him as if he was an 8-year-old and I blushed over how my son was powerless when lying on his chest. He would almost instantly fall asleep in the comfort of his father's arms.

MEMOIRS OF ALMOST BARREN WOMEN:
OUR JOURNEY TO MOTHERHOOD

Let's go back a little, I sort of jumped the gun and shared the successful birth of my son and missed the opportunity to share my journey to successfully becoming pregnant.

There were several years of marital intimacy without contraceptives and no pregnancies. There was over two years of the infamous questions, "When are you guys going to have kids?" "I need you two to have some babies" or "don't wait too long."

To be honest the 1st three years or so, give or take 6 months, we just weren't ready. We talked about it from time to time, and we simply wanted to spend time getting to know each other and traveling. Getting to know each other without the distractions of being parents would prove integral to the strength and longevity of our marriage.

I don't think our waiting contributed to infertility in any way and I appreciate the time we had to get to know each other and navigate the terrains of a new marriage. The good, the bad and the ugly. We allowed each other and ourselves to grow in love in marriage. We got a lot of kinks out that allowed us to be mature unselfish parents.

When my son turned three, I stopped birth control and awaited a wanted pregnancy. Nothing happened and my husband and I previously agreed we would not pay for or go through fertility treatment again.

I didn't enjoy the countless doctors' appointments, the anxiety, and to me the worst part of it all was taking the medications that led to menopausal symptoms and doing self-injections.

MEMOIRS OF ALMOST BARREN WOMEN:
OUR JOURNEY TO MOTHERHOOD

The medications I took, which the doctor warned would take me through symptoms of menopause like moodiness and hot flashes, were a hot mess. I would forget about the effects of the medicine while out and about or visiting family and friends. I would often react loudly and dramatically only to remember mid-way through that this was supposed to happen, and nobody knew I was receiving fertility treatments.

I would flail about and throw my head and arms back until the flash subsided and then I would catch myself and try to get myself together. Looking around I wondered if they thought I was crazy or would question what I was experiencing being too young for menopause.

Then there was the fear of handling syringes full of medication. Aware of the cost and the importance of administering it correctly and in a timely manner made it more painstaking. In addition, injecting myself with needles in my stomach for one medication and then in my thigh for another never felt good. In fact, it often made me feel uncomfortable and I resented it.

This was a large part of why we agreed to avoid fertility treatments in the future. However, when my son was about 6 years old, he began to ask for a sibling. He asked regularly and with great desire. I too wanted another child and no longer forbade fertility care. We were financially stable, and I knew we could make it work.

I discussed it with my husband and he eventually agreed on visiting a fertility specialist to investigate our current situation. Again, I only told one person, and was still limited in what I shared. I was limited in what I really felt.

MEMOIRS OF ALMOST BARREN WOMEN:
OUR JOURNEY TO MOTHERHOOD

In truth I was desperate with a deep desire to have another child. I wanted it for me. I wanted it for my son and I thought it would enrich my family.

I thought of how meaningful it would be for my son to have a sibling. I recalled all the richness provided to me by having multiple siblings. I thought of the many ways we supported each other along the way and always had someone to experience life with.

I wanted that for my child. I feared him being alone and being lonely. I wondered how he would navigate life should something happen to his parents. I wanted to provide comfort and support to him via a sibling.

In regards to my fertility specialist visits, things were going great again. If you can call anything related to being at a fertility doctor great. Things were very optimal. Again the doctors warned me at my initial visits that my age may drastically affect my fertility possibilities. However, after multiple visits we received surprisingly positive results. My ovaries were intact. My eggs were plentiful, I was ovulating regularly, and my labs were great. Now it was time to complete the hysterosalpingogram (HSG).

I recall completing this previously. My sister accompanied me, and I had not taken any pain reducers previously. It hurt. I mean it really hurt. Thankfully, it did not take long. It was this test then and now that sealed my fate. I was then and still was infertile due to the blocking of fallopian tubes. My husband's viable sperm could not use the gateway that was my fallopian tubes to get to my eggs and impregnate them.

MEMOIRS OF ALMOST BARREN WOMEN:
OUR JOURNEY TO MOTHERHOOD

I am not sure if it was age or the fact that I was alone the second time around, but this hurt a lot more. I remember feeling as if a sharp pain came out of nowhere and then that same pain twisted into a knot. It was just horrible. Fortunately, the provider was very caring, personable, and talked and comforted me throughout the procedure. I was told the results right away. Even though I knew the results, it hurt to hear the words.

I kept my composure until I got into the bathroom. It was there that I wept. I can still feel the despair in my hurt, the turning in my belly, and the warmth of the tears running down my face.

I wanted to cry out. I wanted to scream and punch, but I was in a public facility. As I heard the provider yell are "you okay?" I sucked it up. I got it together and replied solemnly, "Yes I am okay." I was not. I knew I wasn't believable, but she and I knew I was doing what I had to. I had to move on.

After this test, my husband and I went into a follow up consultation. The provider reviewed all the tests, was optimistic, and was ready to move on to fertility treatments. She was sure that I could become pregnant with the help of IVF due to my mostly promising results and history.

I too was optimistic and hopeful. It was only then when my husband revealed he was not on board. He still did not want to commit and agreed to full IVF. He cited the cost, the fact that my son was so independent, and he did not want to endure the challenges that a newborn baby brings.

MEMOIRS OF ALMOST BARREN WOMEN:
OUR JOURNEY TO MOTHERHOOD

To say I was hurt and upset would be an understatement. I was angry, furious, frustrated and confused. I wondered and asked why he let me do so much if this was his stance on the topic. Long story short there wasn't a satisfying answer.

I conceded. I didn't want to force my desires on him. I didn't want to disrupt our happy home. I would never forgive myself if this changed the trajectory of our happy marriage. Even worse, I couldn't fathom the thought of bringing an unwanted child into the world. Or having to bear the brunt of parenting because I wanted to have another child and he did not.

Of course, I don't know if any of this would have happened, but the possibility was enough for me. I truly did and do have a great marriage, a peaceful home, and an awesome child. I would never willingly jeopardize that and with all that in mind, I put my desire to have a second child aside and moved on at least in action, but not in desire.

CHAPTER 06

Releasing the Shame

MEMOIRS OF ALMOST BARREN WOMEN:
OUR JOURNEY TO MOTHERHOOD

> Shame should be reserved for the things we choose to do, not the circumstances that life puts on us.
>
> **ANN PATCHETT**

Your story could be totally different from mine. Your fertility journey may not mirror the summary shared by others, however, one thing we have in common is the desire to conceive, deliver a healthy baby, and become a mother/parent.

There are many "whys" behind what has led each of us on this journey, but we do not have to live in shame and/or blame. We can pivot and fulfill our desires through different channels. I am not saying I should give up or opt out of parenting. For each of us, that time and decision is personal and individualized.

You may choose from a variety of fertility support, you may choose to foster and later adopt, or you may decide to parent indirectly through God's children, nieces and nephews, or help children who are less fortunate or mentoring.

What I am saying is deciding to accept life's challenges without allowing the pitfalls to consume us is pivotal. It may hurt and there may be many days of anguish, but you can and will get through this. Be careful of comparison, guilt, and envy.

They are joy killers.

MEMOIRS OF ALMOST BARREN WOMEN:
OUR JOURNEY TO MOTHERHOOD

You are not alone. You do not have to allow this to define you or your self-worth. Let's take a look at shame. It is an unpleasant self-conscious emotion typically associated with a negative evaluation of self; withdrawal of motivations; and feelings of distress, exposure, mistrust, powerlessness, and worthlessness (Wikipedia Contributors, 2020). It goes on to say shame causes people to hide and is dysfunctional. To add to that shame is the painful feeling arising from the consciousness of something dishonorable, improper, and ridiculous, etc., done by oneself or another (Dictionary.com, 2020).

Even if this is how you feel or have felt, you don't want to stay there. I would be lying if I never felt shame. In fact, it is the shame that has kept me silent for so long. It is the shame that allowed me to only reveal part of my heart regarding my desire to have a baby and the related challenges.

Shame may have even led to me not progressing to motherhood quicker, motherhood for a second time, and sharing my journey so openly and honestly. These examples alone highlight why we must drop shame and pick-up joy, hope, honesty, transparency, and the option to choose.

Choose what path you want to take, choose happiness, choose to release all guilt, shame, and choose your peace. I am imploring you to release shame and guilt as soon as possible. Use your inner strength to decide to be happy despite your circumstances. Find connections to things that drive your joy and allow you to utilize those inherent nurturing desires to bless the lives of others and you will see it will enrich and bless your life as well.

Remember, decision making is up to you and your family alone. Do not feel pressured by your family, age, or your friends' paths or timelines. Instead, explore your options when you are ready to investigate other paths.

MEMOIRS OF ALMOST BARREN WOMEN:
OUR JOURNEY TO MOTHERHOOD

My goal is to say **it is okay!** There is no shame! Release the guilt and celebrate your different paths to parenthood when you are ready! Being ready is important. None of these paths are easy. Most of them have a lot of red tape and steps to completion and success.

In doing all this, exercise self-care by ensuring you are emotionally and mentally ready for the twist turns and bumps. I am bold enough to say having a child is worth the process, but it is not worth your mental health and peace. If you are disrupted mentally, spiritually, and physically by all of this, take a step back and take the time to restore you and your family to wholeness.

Ensuring total wellness within your capabilities while navigating your journey to parenthood is integral to equipping you and your spouse, partner, or family through what can be a strenuous and lengthy process.

Also remember, you are not some weird anomaly. This is not a rare condition that 1 in 1000 families experience. The truth is approximately one in ten families have some type of infertility challenge. New reports from the CDC suggest as many as one in seven families have some sort of infertility challenge.

From miscarriages and stillbirths to never getting pregnant, many other women have had similar experiences. Begin talking to those around you to learn more and grow your support system.

I am confident that just like me once you open up you will learn more and find more families who too are going through this journey. Hopefully this will allow you to have someone to experience this with, learn from, or help

MEMOIRS OF ALMOST BARREN WOMEN:
OUR JOURNEY TO MOTHERHOOD

along their journey.

For example, when I was beginning my fertility treatment, I ran into a family member who was also starting infertility care. I remember not wanting anyone to know why I was there as I visited my local hospital where many people in my community worked and sought care.

However, I ran into this family member and although I felt that initial pang of embarrassment, we went on to share our stories with one another and supported each other along the way.

We exchanged numbers and went on to be there for one another through every step.

Her story was different than mine. She was married and started infertility care along with her husband, but along the way the relationship dissolved, her spouse didn't support the process anymore and she was left still wanting to be a mother but having to do it alone. Prior to her marriage dissolving she was informed that she too had scarred fallopian tubes and decided to attempt to remove the scarring and try to get pregnant without IVF.

After they parted ways, she made the courageous choice to continue infertility care alone. She opted to use donor sperm and become a single parent. Although she began infertility treatment before me, she ran into a few more roadblocks. The loss of her relationship, and then something didn't go as planned along the way.

MEMOIRS OF ALMOST BARREN WOMEN:
OUR JOURNEY TO MOTHERHOOD

I cannot recall clearly if it was her egg retrieval, her transfer, or deciding on her donor. These are just a few of the many hurdles women and families have to traverse.

The moral of this chapter is that neither of us had many allies during this time. We were scared and didn't have much knowledge or support initially. We were not comfortable sharing and did not know who we could trust and be vulnerable with. We were left to face these emotions, make these decisions, and absorb these fears and disappointments all alone until we connected. Make a connection with a support group as well as someone you can be fully transparent with. It will make the difference.

If you are that support person, be intentional in your conversations. Be sure not to compare or minimize the journey. It is a big burden to bear and every detail is weighty. Ask questions, offer support, and be the respite they need along the way.

MEMOIRS OF ALMOST BARREN WOMEN:
OUR JOURNEY TO MOTHERHOOD

Lindsey's Journey

Going to a fertility doctor makes you feel like you are broken, so broken that it should be kept secret.

MEMOIRS OF ALMOST BARREN WOMEN:
OUR JOURNEY TO MOTHERHOOD

We spend so much of our lives trying NOT to get pregnant, so why is it that when we want to, we can't? In 2010, I became pregnant with my first born, and to be honest, my husband and I don't really recall "when" it actually happened. We were in our twenties and many of our friends were getting married that year, so let's just say we had a lot of fun and next thing we knew, we were pregnant!

Fast forward to 2015, when we consciously decided we wanted a baby, of course, the stars just didn't align. We tried for a year, unsuccessfully on our own and then decided that the next step was a fertility doctor. For us, this was a very hard thing to do. It was hard because you have to admit to yourself that something might be wrong with one or even both of you. I remember going to the doctor's office and thinking to myself "I hope I don't see anyone I know!" Like many others going to a fertility doctor makes you feel like you are broken. So broken that it should be kept secret. To my surprise, it's actually an incredibly common thing. Now that I've gone through all of this I am at a point that I'm comfortable sharing my story. I realize that it touches more people than I ever would have imagined. I tell you that so you know...**you're not alone**.

The first plan at a fertility doctor of course is to find out what's not working. I remember sitting in the waiting room thinking, is it him? Is it me? It's got to just be some weird fluke, like, our timing is just off, right? And then come the tests, tests on me, tests on him, tests, tests, tests! It's exhausting. Let's take a minute to rewind. When I had my first born, I ended up getting MRSA in my C-section incision and had twelve weeks of in-home nursing care because the infection was so bad. I was in so much pain that I had to sleep in one of those recliners that will stand you all the way up (because I couldn't actually do that on my own).

MEMOIRS OF ALMOST BARREN WOMEN:
OUR JOURNEY TO MOTHERHOOD

I was lucky enough that my parents had one of those recliners from when they were taking care of my grandfather. So, the moment I tell the fertility doctor I had MRSA, he orders a laparoscopy to see how much damage has been done. Damage confirmed, and to add to it, the doctor also confirmed I had endometriosis, but not so bad that I shouldn't be able to get pregnant, he shared. So, I started taking the hormones to help us out and tried intrauterine insemination (IUI). Fast forward to waiting to hear the results from the doctor. It is enough torture taking a home pregnancy test, let alone waiting for a call back from a doctor! Nothing, I mean nothing got done that day at work! The next thing I know, my phone rings and I immediately recognize the number. It's the fertility doctor. When I answer with, "hello," the world stops, "This is the doctor's office, we received your pregnancy test results back" the next statement felt like it took an eternity to come out of her mouth, "Congratulations, YOU'RE PREGNANT!!"

I couldn't believe it, the day was finally here! After almost a year and a half, we were finally pregnant! I immediately called my husband and we celebrated over the phone, starting to think through how we were going to tell our families. It was a moment filled with pure joy. After I hung up with him I remember sitting quietly trying to let it all sink in with a million thoughts racing through my mind. And then, my phone rang again. It was the doctor's office, again. "Hi, it's Sarah from the doctor's office," she paused. "I'm so sorry, but I read your test results wrong. It was a false positive." I sat silently in shock while she said, "I'm so very sorry." This news was absolutely devastating, to the point that we decided maybe the time wasn't right for us, so we took a little break and then went back to the old-fashioned way of trying on our own.

MEMOIRS OF ALMOST BARREN WOMEN:
OUR JOURNEY TO MOTHERHOOD

In late 2016, we decided we would try again, but got a recommendation from an acquaintance for a different doctor this time. We went for a consultation and basically decided to go big or go home. We were going to try in vitro fertilization (IVF) and let me tell you, it's a commitment. After going to appointments on an incredibly regular basis and all the details that go along with it, we found ourselves, again, waiting for THAT call. I remember the phone ringing and feeling absolutely terrified that the answer was again going to be no. I answered and got a very similar message as before, "Congratulations, you are pregnant!"

But this time, I held off my excitement. "Are you sure," I said. "Yes ma'am, you're pregnant!" "I hear you," I said, "but what are the chances you're wrong? I've had someone tell me this before and they were wrong, and..." I went on and on and on. The woman on the other end assured me that my test was a true positive and I couldn't believe my ears. It was weird because, I expected after all that time that I would be through the roof ecstatic, but there was something holding me back, something that made me feel scared. Thinking back, when I found out I was pregnant with my first, I recall having a very similar feeling.

That overwhelming feeling of deep responsibility, of importance, of... you can't mess this up, this is someone's life we are talking about! I think we all have our own way of dealing with things and our own set of emotions based on what life has given us. I came around and once it sunk in, I was elated, but I think we all have somewhat of an "oh shit" moment when we find out we are bringing another life into the world.

MEMOIRS OF ALMOST BARREN WOMEN:
OUR JOURNEY TO MOTHERHOOD

May 17, 2018 our not so little 10lb, almost 24 inches (yes a two foot tall baby) Camryn came into the world via scheduled C-section. To think that I almost gave up trying to have him because, honestly, infertility is hard! It's really hard! I know its cliché, but I really can't imagine my world without him. He is a natural comedian; he loves to snuggle. When he sits next to you, he has to be touching. He loves his big brother and everything his big brother does and never forgets to grab one for his "Bubba" when he grabs himself a snack. It was really a very painful road to get him here on earth, but the process has changed me and has me appreciate the things that I have in life.

Lindsey

CHAPTER 07

Lessons Learned

MEMOIRS OF ALMOST BARREN WOMEN:
OUR JOURNEY TO MOTHERHOOD

> And sometimes against all odds, against all logic, we still hope.
>
> **UNKNOWN**

It is hard to have hope when you are in despair and you want something so desperately, but hope is just that. Hope is a desire for something that is not. Something that you feel will make things better. Often times, it is something we do not have the power alone to possess and that makes things more difficult.

Can you imagine if we had all the power, resources, and finances to remedy our fertility struggles? If we could easily produce the money, the doctor could perform the procedure or prescribe the medication, or have the miracle just appear. For many of us, this isn't happening. Instead, we have to tighten up and endure the hurdles and challenges that come along with this dreaded diagnosis.

Fortunately, times are changing, and we do not have to do it alone. There are more resources, funding, and understanding than ever before. Is it at overwhelming numbers, no. Is it always obvious? No. Is it even comfortable? Heck no! However, more and more awareness over the years has led to more large companies including it in their benefits packages. There is more research and news articles. Research and funding options are growing etc.

On a more granular level, every day people are more apt to discuss it. You can check Instagram and find quite a few fertility pages or people who share their stories and journey. Please beware that there are others who

MEMOIRS OF ALMOST BARREN WOMEN:
OUR JOURNEY TO MOTHERHOOD

share in a way that can be uncomfortable and can seem callous or triggering. Each of us cope and share differently. I am sure the off-colored jokes or the sarcasm of some of these pages is an effort to reduce the sting and release some steam. As you traverse these pages, be aware of this and quickly unfollow or click away if this disrupts your soul.

What I have found is that although people are uncomfortable, they really want to talk about it. They want a safe space, and they want to have these conversations with people who understand. We don't want the pity of those who have never experienced this. We don't want the obligatory, "Oh that is okay, at least you have _____ (insert that thing you have but will never replace the desire to have a child or more children)."

That's right! Money, material things, and career are not the gap fillers for having a baby. We want those too and we appreciate them, but we want a baby or babies, and we don't want to sacrifice one for the other. We are able to manage careers, education, entrepreneurship and mothering/parenting.

Let's face it, oftentimes people do not know what to say. Lack of knowledge, experience, and awareness are usually the contributing factors. With that in mind we can choose to give our well-meaning family, friends, and coworkers grace and space and room to grow.

I know many of us would love to sprinkle something on the head of these people when they mention, blurt out, or ask about triggering things related to our lack of children. Or is it just me hoping to shrink their heads like Beetlejuice? Instead, I had to garner the courage to share with those I wanted to share with and educate with kindness. Most of the time this quieted the countless inquiries of "When are you going to have a baby?" Or statements like, "You have everything else it's time to have a child."

I have had to share many times that I cannot have kids without fertility treatment and my husband, and I have decided we would stop at one. I have also shared, "I am not preventing pregnancy. I just have not gotten pregnant."

Before having my son, I had to tell a friend who helped to spread the word that I wished people would stop asking me. I was uncomfortable, and I also felt pressured and stressed. People began to understand, and the inquiries stopped.

It may take some courageous conversations, but it will decrease the inquiries, awkward moments, and more people will begin to understand.

If you have gotten this far it is highly likely you are on a journey to become a mother. Mothering is defined by Cambridge dictionary as the process of caring for children or caring for people in a way a mother does (Cambridge University Press, 2021).

Some common options for mothering/parenting are:

Journey to Parenthood Options*:

- Embryo adoption/Donor eggs
- Gestational surrogacy
- In vitro fertilization
- Egg freezing
- Foster care
- Adoption

> I think it's very important whenever we talk about fertility and infertility to include foster parenting and adoption as well because biology is oftentimes the least of what makes someone a parent,
>
> **ASHTON SAID (KINDELAN, TANG, & LINENDOLL, 2019).**

Indirect Parenting Options:

- Mentoring
- Coaching
- Daycare Provider

*Be aware of your different state laws and policies. For example, gestational surrogacy is not legal in all states. As I was writing I learned that it recently became legal in New York. Prior to that, families were left to explore other options or seek surrogacy out of state. When utilizing a surrogate, even if it is a close friend or family member. It is integral to have a lawyer represent both sides and document the processes, agreements, and rights of all parties.

Keep in mind, overall, most people do care. Inform your close circle of your journey and be unashamed. Help them understand that for many of us it isn't that easy to just get pregnant.

MEMOIRS OF ALMOST BARREN WOMEN:
OUR JOURNEY TO MOTHERHOOD

It is not always so simple to carry a baby to full term, and it outright hurts to lose a child at any stage and it's not any easier to never be able to get pregnant with or without fertility care. This can be true for either married or single people wanting to bear, carry, and raise their own child. More people need to know of our struggles and our story. Optimally their unknowing will go from probing quests to heartfelt prayers and support.

Conclusion

MEMOIRS OF ALMOST BARREN WOMEN:
OUR JOURNEY TO MOTHERHOOD

> Infertility is one of the most draining and dream shattering experiences to have to endure
>
> But infertility will not win
>
> And we will do more than just endure
>
> We will bravely and boldly bloom
>
> **TIM CELESTE JR**

No matter where you are in this journey, my hope for you is joy, contentment and peace. I also hope your journey ends with the loving family your heart desires. Had I not sought and received IVF I would not have had the witty, silly, loving boy who continues to motivate me to be the best for him, myself, and the world.

I encourage you to be open to different approaches, methods, and opportunities to start your family. If you are not there yet examine why. If it's lack of knowledge, begin your research. If it's lack of support, expand your support system. This will definitely require being open to sharing with more people and/or joining support groups in person or via social media. If its finances explore you or your spouse's employee benefits. Many companies have some sort of benefit that assist with adoption and infertility care. For example, companies like Bank of America, Tesla and Spotify have unlimited IVF coverage. It is amazing knowing that many of us would require more than one cycle of IVF to conceive one or more children. Even some of our favorite brands have great IVF benefits like Starbucks and Chobani.

In 2019, companies like ExxonMobil, AT&T, Procter and Gamble, Liberty Mutual, Tyson Foods, Northwestern Mutual, General Mills, and Geico introduced or dramatically upgraded their fertility benefits (The Fertility IQ Family Builder Workplace Index: 2019 – 2020, 2021).

MEMOIRS OF ALMOST BARREN WOMEN:
OUR JOURNEY TO MOTHERHOOD

If your company is a private insurer, they may not cover infertility treatment. You still have options. Look into your local fertility clinic they often have grant monies or discount programs. There are also many foundations who have monies to give to families looking to begin IVF but don't have the resources. Be prepared for long applications that may require you to provide details about your journey, finances, and health.

You can have peace and contentment and still long and desire to begin or grow your family. Believe me, I'm living it. I'm grateful for my life and the amazing things God, my career, and my spouse have provided. I am beyond blessed to have a son born after one successful IVF transfer. He is healthy, strong, caring, creative and charismatic.

He and I both desire a sibling for him. I planned as a young lady to have two kids three or five years a part. In hopes they would avoid being in the same life and development stages. When my son turned three, I stopped birth control in hopes I'd get pregnant again without the help of IVF. At that time my husband and I were on the same page.

We were happy with one, would not do IVF again, and if we were to have another child it would happen naturally. Needless to say as I was writing this book my son was nine and since given birth in 2011 I have not gotten pregnant again. When my boy was six or seven years old I convinced my husband to revisit IVF again. He reluctantly agreed, but unbeknownst to me we were not on the same page this time. I was excited and looking forward to another successful round.

We were referred to an excellent fertility group in our area and at each visit the staff from check in to check out was great. The process and results

MEMOIRS OF ALMOST BARREN WOMEN:
OUR JOURNEY TO MOTHERHOOD

were similar. My eggs were surprisingly more than expected and viable. Labs were good, cycle good and after another painful HSG I learned my fallopian tubes were completely blocked. I was more upset this time than the first time.

Shortly after that study, my husband and I returned to the clinic for a discussion with the doctor. Overall, she was pleased with my results and she wanted to move forward and exclaimed I was a good candidate.

It wasn't until that day my husband shared; he was not on board. I was devastated crushed to say the least. I was even angry that he'd withheld his true feelings. He didn't want to go through the process, didn't want to pay the money, and frankly was content and didn't want to do "the baby thing again."

I was crushed to say the least. My son was disappointed and didn't fully understand. After all he saw all of our friends and family members continue to get pregnant and bring more babies into the family.

I share because I know I am not alone. I know many women and families share similarities to my story or the other women who unselfishly shared their story in this memoir. Life's circumstances are not always what we desire. However, we must keep hope and joy in our lives.

Together we can support one another. We can share our stories and our resources to comfort, educate, and inspire others. Let's make infertility discussions more common and make alternate ways to parenting normal. It does not make our kids any less ours. Even if they do not look like us, we do not share the same DNA, or if we do not carry them in our womb.

MEMOIRS OF ALMOST BARREN WOMEN:
OUR JOURNEY TO MOTHERHOOD

We are bonded through our nurturing and love. We are connected through our family morals, values, and memories. Our family is just that ours. No one can take that away from us. If you mother/parent them they are yours and you have the honor of caring and raising them to be amazing.

Wishing you peace and freedom from guilt or shame as you undertake your own journey to parenthood.

Signed almost barren but not broken,

Tanerra

MEMOIRS OF ALMOST BARREN WOMEN:
OUR JOURNEY TO MOTHERHOOD

In writing this book I learned of many celebrities or influencers who have bravely shared their journeys. I share some of their names with the intent it helps you to feel less isolated, ashamed, and unique.

- Amy Schumer
- Anne Hathaway
- Angela Bassett
- Beyoncé
- Bill Rancic
- Celine Dion
- Chrissy Tiegan
- Christina Perri
- Courtney Cox
- Eve Jihan Jeffers Cooper
- Gabrielle Douglas
- Gordon Ramsey
- Hugh Jackman
- Kim Kardashian
- Maria Menounos
- Mariah Carey
- Michelle Obama
- Rachel Dugen
- Sharon Osbourne
- Tamron Hall
- Tia Mowry-Hardrict
- Tyra Banks

MEMOIRS OF ALMOST BARREN WOMEN:
OUR JOURNEY TO MOTHERHOOD

Did you notice the low number of men on this list? It is not because they don't exist. Because it is still unspoken, there is still shame and we have not made it a safe space to share. Let's normalize talking about infertility. Doing so will allow those of use experiencing it to have a greater support system and less grief.

Awareness will grow and resources will follow.

Resources

MEMOIRS OF ALMOST BARREN WOMEN:
OUR JOURNEY TO MOTHERHOOD

Suggested Instagram Accounts to Follow

- @Hopeovertherainbow
- @Fertilitypositive
- @Pregnantish
- @NatalieCrawfordMD
- @BlackGirlsGuidetoFertility
- @Babyquestgrants
- @Fertilitywithinreach
- @Ffcghope
- @Brokenbrownegg
- @Infertilitystories
- @Infertilityandmepodcast
- @Smartpcoschoices
- @Hilariously_infertile
- @Thefertilitykitchen
- @Cadefoundation
- @Resolveorg
- @Mansivfview
- @Sistersinloss

Disclaimer

    The above social media accounts and the following resources are not affiliated with this book, the author, nor the contributors. None of the above mentioned parties are paid to endorse or share this information. Following, engaging, or seeking support and resources from any of these are at the readers discretion.

Websites Supporting Fertility/Parenting/Loss of a pregnancy/Male Infertility

1. Tinina Q. Cade Foundation
   https://cadefoundation.org/

2. Sister Girl Foundation
   https://www.sister-girl.org/

3. The Broken Brown Egg
   https://thebrokenbrownegg.org/

4. Fertility for Colored Girls
   https://www.fertilityforcoloredgirls.org/*

5. RADfertility
   https://radfertility.com/

6. National Council for Adoption
   https://www.adoptioncouncil.org/

7. GoStork
   https://www.gostork.com/our-story

8. American Society for Reproductive Medicine
   https://www.reproductivefacts.org/

9. Society for Assisted ReproductiveTechnology
   https://www.sart.org/

10. **Verywellfamily**
    https://www.verywellfamily.com/

11. **Pregnancy After Loss Support (PALS)**
    https://pregnancyafterlosssupport.org/find-support/

12. **The Yellow Cape (endometriosis support)**
    https://www.theyellowcape.com/

13. **Fertility IQ**
    https://www.fertilityiq.com/

14. **Resolve (resource for males)**
    https://resolve.org/infertility-101/medical-conditions/male-factor/

15. **RMA (resource for males)**
    https://rmanetwork.com/male-infertility/

16. **Fertility Health (resource for males)**
    https://www.genesisfertility.com/blog/infertility-in-celebrities-lessons-learned-by-men/

Financial Resources for Fertility Treatment

1. **Win Fertility**
   https://www.winfertility.com/

2. **Arc Fertility**
   https://www.arcfertility.com/

3. **Lives Stong**
   https://www.livestrong.org/we-can-help/livestrong-fertility

4. **The Fertility for Colored Girls Gift of Hope**
   https://www.fertilityforcoloredgirls.org/gift-of-hope

5. **Baby Quest Foundation Grants**
   https://babyquestfoundation.org/applying-for-a-grant/

6. **Capex MD**
   http://www.capexmd.com/

7. **Prosper Health Care Lending**
   https://www.prosper.com/healthcare-financing

8. **Resolve National Infertility Association**
   https://resolve.org/

9. **Footprints of Angels**
   https://www.footprintsofangels.org/

10. **Starfish Infertility Foundation Braxton Grant**
    https://starfishinfertilityfoundation.org/

Terms and Definitions

- **Pelvic adhesions** bands of scar tissue that bind organs that can form after pelvic infection, appendicitis, endometriosis or abdominal or pelvic surgery
- **Endometriosis** A painful condition in which tissue from the lining of the uterus grows outside of the uterus
- **Fecundity(n)** the ability to produce an abundance of offspring or new growth
- **Fibroids** noncancerous uterine growths
- **Gestational Surrogacy** the child is not biologically related to the **surrogate mother**, who is often referred to as a **gestational** carrier. Instead, the embryo is created via in vitro fertilization (IVF), using the eggs and sperm of the intended parents or donors, and is then transferred to the surrogate
- **Hysterosalpingogram** An X-ray which involves injecting dye through the cervix into the uterus to determine if the fallopian tubes are open and the uterine cavity is normal
- **In Vitro Fertilization (IVF)** An assisted reproductive technique that involves removing sperm and eggs, fertilizing them in a laboratory, then placing a fertilized egg in the uterus
- **Male Factor Infertility** When the cause of a couple's infertility is due to problems in the man or when it contributes to existing fertility problems in the woman
- **Morphology** The size and shape of sperm
- **Motility** The ability of sperm to move by themselves
- **Oligospermia** When a man has too few sperm to fertilize an egg normal

MEMOIRS OF ALMOST BARREN WOMEN:
OUR JOURNEY TO MOTHERHOOD

- **PCOS** multiple small cysts which line the ovaries; A common hormonal condition in which an imbalance in the sex hormones may cause menstrual abnormalities, skin and hair changes, obesity, infertility
- **Uterine Polyps** small growths on the inside of a woman's womb or uterus the can lead to cancer, infertility, heavy periods
- **Preimplantation Genetic Counseling** enables informed decisions for families with a history of genetic disease(s) to have the opportunity to identify which embryos do not carry genetic diseases
- **Reproductive Endocrinologist** a physician specializing and endocrinology and gynecology who diagnoses and treats endocrine disorders that are either directly or indirectly related to reproduction and infertility
- **Selective Reduction** abortion of one or more but not all embryos in a pregnancy with multiple embryos
- **Semen Analysis** evaluates the quality, movement, and form or structure of the sperm
- **Sonohysterogram** Ultrasound to evaluate the uterus for fibroids and/or polyps

* This list in no way an all-inclusive list of words and treatments of infertility. Instead, it is a compilation of many of the related terms or shared issues used in this memoir.

Works Cited

MEMOIRS OF ALMOST BARREN WOMEN:
OUR JOURNEY TO MOTHERHOOD

One. American Heritage Idioms Dictionary. (2020). Shame. Retrieved from Dictionary.com:
https://www.dictionary.com/browse/shame
Houghton Mifflin Harcourt Publishing Company.

Two. Cambridge University Press. (2021, January 9). Cambridge Dictionary. Retrieved from https://dictionary.cambridge.org/us/:
https://dictionary.cambridge.org/us/dictionary/english/mothering

Three. Carnes, A. (2017, November 8). Tech Firms Get High Marks for Covering Infertility treatments. New York Times, Late . New York, New York, United States.

Four. Fertility for Colored Girls. (2020, October 10). Retrieved from FertilityforColoredgirls.org:
https://www.fertilityforcoloredgirls.org/

Five. Genesis Fertility and Reproductive Medicine. (2019, February 28). Infertility in Celebrities – Lessons learned by Men. Retrieved from
https://www.genesisfertility.com

Six. Kindelan, K., Tang, E., and Linendoll, W. (2019, April 23). The ABCs of infertility: Here's how people are getting pregnant in 2019.

Seven. Mayo Clinic. (2020, November 2). Infertility. Retrieved from mayoclinic.org:
https://www.mayoclinic.org/diseases-conditions/infertility

Eight. Peterson, B. (2018). Five Myths about Infertility . The Washington Post.

MEMOIRS OF ALMOST BARREN WOMEN:
OUR JOURNEY TO MOTHERHOOD

Nine.   The FertilityIQ Family Builder Workplace Index: 2019 - 2020. (2021, January 9). Retrieved from Fertility IQ: https://www.fertilityiq.com/topics/ivf/the-fertilityiq-family-builder-workplace-index-2019-2020

Ten.   USA.gov. (2020, October 30). Reproductive Health: Infertility . Retrieved from Centers for Disease Control and Prevention: https://www.cdc.gov/reproductivehealth/infertility/index.htm

Eleven.   Wikepedia (2020, December 22). Shame. Wikipedia The Free Encyclopedia . Retrieved from: https://en.wikipedia.org/wiki/Shame. Wikimedia Foundation, Inc.

Journal

My Journey to Parenthood Journal

Today I am

Message of Hope

Today's Self-care Activity

THOUGHTS, PRAYERS & NOTES

....

....

....

....

....

....

....

....

....

My Journey to Parenthood Journal

Today I am

Message of Hope

Today's Self-care Activity

THOUGHTS, PRAYERS & NOTES

My Journey to Parenthood Journal

Today I am

Message of Hope

Today's Self-care Activity

THOUGHTS, PRAYERS & NOTES

My Journey to Parenthood Journal

Today I am

Message of Hope

Today's Self-care Activity

THOUGHTS, PRAYERS & NOTES

My Journey to
Parenthood Journal

Today I am

Message of Hope

Today's Self-care Activity

THOUGHTS, PRAYERS & NOTES

My Journey to Parenthood Journal

Today I am

Message of Hope

Today's Self-care Activity

THOUGHTS, PRAYERS & NOTES

My Journey to Parenthood Journal

Today I am

Message of Hope

Today's Self-care Activity

THOUGHTS, PRAYERS & NOTES

My Journey to Parenthood Journal

Today I am

Message of Hope

Today's Self-care Activity

THOUGHTS, PRAYERS & NOTES

My Journey to Parenthood Journal

Today I am

Message of Hope

Today's Self-care Activity

THOUGHTS, PRAYERS & NOTES

My Journey to Parenthood Journal

Today I am

Message of Hope

Today's Self-care Activity

THOUGHTS, PRAYERS & NOTES

My Journey to Parenthood Journal

Today I am

Message of Hope

Today's Self-care Activity

THOUGHTS, PRAYERS & NOTES

....

....

....

....

....

....

....

....

....

My Journey to Parenthood Journal

Today I am

Message of Hope

Today's Self-care Activity

THOUGHTS, PRAYERS & NOTES

My Journey to Parenthood Journal

Today I am

> [ ]

Message of Hope

> [ ]

Today's Self-care Activity

> [ ]

THOUGHTS, PRAYERS & NOTES

....
....
....
....
....
....
....
....
....

My Journey to Parenthood Journal

Today I am

Message of Hope

Today's Self-care Activity

THOUGHTS, PRAYERS & NOTES

My Journey to Parenthood Journal

Today I am

[ ]

Message of Hope

[ ]

Today's Self-care Activity

[ ]

THOUGHTS, PRAYERS & NOTES

....

....

....

....

....

....

....

....

My Journey to Parenthood Journal

Today I am

Message of Hope

Today's Self-care Activity

THOUGHTS, PRAYERS & NOTES

My Journey to Parenthood Journal

Today I am

Message of Hope

Today's Self-care Activity

THOUGHTS, PRAYERS & NOTES

My Journey to Parenthood Journal

Today I am

Message of Hope

Today's Self-care Activity

THOUGHTS, PRAYERS & NOTES

My Journey to Parenthood Journal

Today I am

Message of Hope

Today's Self-care Activity

THOUGHTS, PRAYERS & NOTES

My Journey to Parenthood Journal

Today I am

Message of Hope

Today's Self-care Activity

THOUGHTS, PRAYERS & NOTES

My Journey to Parenthood Journal

Today I am

Message of Hope

Today's Self-care Activity

THOUGHTS, PRAYERS & NOTES

My Journey to Parenthood Journal

Today I am

Message of Hope

Today's Self-care Activity

THOUGHTS, PRAYERS & NOTES

My Journey to Parenthood Journal

Today I am

Message of Hope

Today's Self-care Activity

THOUGHTS, PRAYERS & NOTES

My Journey to Parenthood Journal

Today I am

Message of Hope

Today's Self-care Activity

THOUGHTS, PRAYERS & NOTES

My Journey to Parenthood Journal

Today I am

```
┌─────────────────────────────────────────┐
│                                         │
└─────────────────────────────────────────┘
```

Message of Hope

```
┌─────────────────────────────────────────┐
│                                         │
└─────────────────────────────────────────┘
```

Today's Self-care Activity

```
┌─────────────────────────────────────────┐
│                                         │
└─────────────────────────────────────────┘
```

THOUGHTS, PRAYERS & NOTES

....
....
....
....
....
....
....
....
....
....

My Journey to Parenthood Journal

Today I am

Message of Hope

Today's Self-care Activity

THOUGHTS, PRAYERS & NOTES

My Journey to Parenthood Journal

Today I am

Message of Hope

Today's Self-care Activity

THOUGHTS, PRAYERS & NOTES

....
....
....
....
....
....
....
....
....

My Journey to Parenthood Journal

Today I am

Message of Hope

Today's Self-care Activity

THOUGHTS, PRAYERS & NOTES

My Journey to Parenthood Journal

Today I am

Message of Hope

Today's Self-care Activity

THOUGHTS, PRAYERS & NOTES

....
....
....
....
....
....
....
....
....

My Journey to Parenthood Journal

Today I am

[ ]

Message of Hope

[ ]

Today's Self-care Activity

[ ]

THOUGHTS, PRAYERS & NOTES

....
....
....
....
....
....
....
....

My Journey to Parenthood Journal

Today I am

```
[                                                              ]
```

Message of Hope

```
[                                                              ]
```

Today's Self-care Activity

```
[                                                              ]
```

THOUGHTS, PRAYERS & NOTES

_____

_____

_____

_____

_____

_____

_____

_____

_____

_____

My Journey to Parenthood Journal

Today I am

Message of Hope

Today's Self-care Activity

THOUGHTS, PRAYERS & NOTES

My Journey to Parenthood Journal

Today I am

Message of Hope

Today's Self-care Activity

THOUGHTS, PRAYERS & NOTES

My Journey to Parenthood Journal

Today I am

Message of Hope

Today's Self-care Activity

THOUGHTS, PRAYERS & NOTES

My Journey to Parenthood Journal

Today I am

Message of Hope

Today's Self-care Activity

THOUGHTS, PRAYERS & NOTES

....
....
....
....
....
....
....
....

My Journey to Parenthood Journal

Today I am

Message of Hope

Today's Self-care Activity

THOUGHTS, PRAYERS & NOTES

My Journey to Parenthood Journal

Today I am

Message of Hope

Today's Self-care Activity

THOUGHTS, PRAYERS & NOTES

....
....
....
....
....
....
....
....

My Journey to Parenthood Journal

Today I am

Message of Hope

Today's Self-care Activity

THOUGHTS, PRAYERS & NOTES

My Journey to Parenthood Journal

Today I am

Message of Hope

Today's Self-care Activity

THOUGHTS, PRAYERS & NOTES

My Journey to Parenthood Journal

Today I am

Message of Hope

Today's Self-care Activity

THOUGHTS, PRAYERS & NOTES

My Journey to
Parenthood Journal

Today I am

[ ]

Message of Hope

[ ]

Today's Self-care Activity

[ ]

THOUGHTS, PRAYERS & NOTES

....

....

....

....

....

....

....

....

My Journey to Parenthood Journal

Today I am

Message of Hope

Today's Self-care Activity

THOUGHTS, PRAYERS & NOTES

My Journey to Parenthood Journal

Today I am

Message of Hope

Today's Self-care Activity

THOUGHTS, PRAYERS & NOTES

My Journey to Parenthood Journal

Today I am

Message of Hope

Today's Self-care Activity

THOUGHTS, PRAYERS & NOTES

My Journey to Parenthood Journal

Today I am

Message of Hope

Today's Self-care Activity

THOUGHTS, PRAYERS & NOTES

....

....

....

....

....

....

....

....

My Journey to Parenthood Journal

Today I am

Message of Hope

Today's Self-care Activity

THOUGHTS, PRAYERS & NOTES

My Journey to Parenthood Journal

Today I am

Message of Hope

Today's Self-care Activity

THOUGHTS, PRAYERS & NOTES

My Journey to Parenthood Journal

Today I am

Message of Hope

Today's Self-care Activity

THOUGHTS, PRAYERS & NOTES

My Journey to Parenthood Journal

Today I am

Message of Hope

Today's Self-care Activity

THOUGHTS, PRAYERS & NOTES

My Journey to Parenthood Journal

Today I am

Message of Hope

Today's Self-care Activity

THOUGHTS, PRAYERS & NOTES

My Journey to Parenthood Journal

Today I am

Message of Hope

Today's Self-care Activity

THOUGHTS, PRAYERS & NOTES

My Journey to Parenthood Journal

Today I am

Message of Hope

Today's Self-care Activity

THOUGHTS, PRAYERS & NOTES

My Journey to Parenthood Journal

Today I am

Message of Hope

Today's Self-care Activity

THOUGHTS, PRAYERS & NOTES

Reviews

MEMOIRS OF ALMOST BARREN WOMEN:
OUR JOURNEY TO MOTHERHOOD

It's captivating, heavy and necessary.

S.F.

Tanerra and all of the contributing authors exposed us to pain, hope, healing and joy unapologetically. The title alone sends a confirming message of hope. These women shared themselves and their journeys. Journeys and experiences that will open the door to conversations, eradicating fear and shame and building a network of supports. His book gently shouts you are not alone! I take my hat off to Tanerra and the contributing authors for their transparency and their truth. These strong women shared in a way that was understandable and digestible. There are so many added benefits to this memoir; the resources, the definitions, the journal. Remarkable work!

KAMELA SMITH

M.ed Public Health Professional

MEMOIRS OF ALMOST BARREN WOMEN:
OUR JOURNEY TO MOTHERHOOD

I thought that the stories in this book were excellent!

As a clinical social worker and an infertility patient, I appreciate the level of honesty and vulnerability that these women share about their journey to build and grow their families. I could follow and identify with their emotional journey that infertility brings for the ride. As a Christian, I also appreciate the palpable sense of hope and faith that each of these women have discussed in their stories. Children are a gift from God, and God's plan for creating our family is the best one. I love that each of their desires to be a mother was the same, even though the path to get there was different. The way these women tell their stories with boldness and courage also speaks to who they are as proud mothers. While their journey to motherhood was not the one they chose, I love how there is not an ounce of regret that any of them have in their story. I highly enjoyed reading this book and would encourage other women who are on their own fertility journey to read this book. This book reminds us that infertility is not a club we choose to be in, but in that club we are not alone in the journey to become mothers.

LG SOCIAL WORKER

MEMOIRS OF ALMOST BARREN WOMEN:
OUR JOURNEY TO MOTHERHOOD

I am currently traversing the fertility journey. And could appreciate every term that was spelled out – particularly about PCOS; the corrective surgery; the discussion around a nutritionist; the description of shame and blame that was felt. All of it, made me feel seen. I identified with EVERY line. To the point I sat on the sofa reading next to my husband and would exclaim "Amens!" and "Wows" out loud. This book felt like a bear hug, and it reminded me of what a friend has shared - that our journeys are never just about us. But always for us to reach back and help someone else along their journey.

CHRISTIAN E GUY

Memoirs of Almost Barren Women, was engaging and insightful. Tanerra and her fellow co-authors give a clear glimpse into the emotions and lives of women who suffer from infertility. Tanerra shares candidly about her past sexual activity and even discloses, in full detail, some of her actions and the guilt she carried for quite some time – even blaming herself at times for her infertility. I admire her courage and transparency. Read the book and pass it on the others.

LISA LEWIS
Seeds of Greatness Bible Church

www.ingramcontent.com/pod-product-compliance
Lightning Source LLC
Chambersburg PA
CBHW072020070526
44583CB00015B/1559